Farewell to Disneyland
My Decade of Young Widowhood

By
Val Chang Snekvik

BOSTON, MASSACHUSETTS

Cover art and design by Susanna Chapman
Book Layout © 2017 BookDesignTemplates.com

Farewell to Disneyland: My Decade of Young Widowhood/ Val Chang Snekvik -- 1st ed.
valchangsnekvik@gmail.com

ISBN 978-0-578-43760-6
Ebook ISBN 978-0-578-43761-3

For Sam, Stephen, and Mark: You three are my heart, walking around town.

And for James: For me, you are the embodiment of the saying, "God makes things new."

"All transitions are composed of an ending, a neutral zone, and a new beginning."

— William Bridges,
The Way of Transition: Embracing Life's Most Difficult Moments

"Unfortunately, when it comes to cancer, American society is far from rational. We are possessed with fear....But it is not only a matter of simple fear: cancer-phobia has expanded into a demonism in which the evil spirit is ever present, but furtively reviewed and spoken of obliquely...American cancer-phobia, in brief, is a disease as serious to society as cancer is to the individual —and morally more devastating."

— F.J. Ingelfinger,
"Cancer! Alarm! Cancer!"
New England Journal of Medicine, Dec 18, 1975

CONTENTS

Introduction

This collection of short chapters spans 2008–2018, the decade during which I became widowed and still went on to wake up the next day. Lots of things can label my experience: numb philosopher, lost other half, manic parent, logistics goddess, weirdly dressed runner, person trying to date while teenage son is also trying to date. I wrote the chapters more or less over the course of five years, starting in 2013. I did skip around in time a little to follow the developments of my headspace and feelings. I added some calendar dates to help you, the reader, locate your spot chronologically.

My title referencing Disneyland came as I finished the chapters and realized that, more than widowhood, this book is about the death of idealism. It's hard to let this go, especially when I come from a background of positive religious faith. I like living with a vision of heaven, love, healing, and trying to be a good neighbor. And even though cancer and crisis years were awful, what's actually been harder is accepting that mediocrity, scars, and plugging along are a big part of life. So, I admit that in writing about changes in my mindset, I am still actively wrestling with how to look at my glass as half full without bemoaning all that empty space.

All events are true to the facts as best as I remember them. The one exception is that when I describe purchasing Andrew's grave plot the day before he died, I ended up calling the cemetery woman "Tabitha." Really, I have no idea what her name was. Sorry, real "Tabitha," you were nice to me and I made light of your garb and demeanor. For most friends, I use their real names if they gave me permission. For enemies, I omitted names or made up substitutes. I take responsibility for any unintended but important omissions, distortions, and errors contained in this memoir.

My choice of pausing the story with my wedding in the summer of 2018 has nothing to do with seeing a finished story tied up with a bow, as though life is now settled with a spouse in my life again. Indeed, life with a midlife partner and older children seems ever more out of my control, not to mention humbling as it kills my assumptions about what should happen and when. The pause in the written account has more to do with my need to live more before I say much more.

A note to those in grief, or any who support them:

During the first stretch of widowhood, I liked two, and only two, grief books. It doesn't really matter what they were because the important thing about them was that a) I could stomach their tone, and b) they each gave me one to two nuggets I could latch onto as life preservers. Many psychologists have written wise and organized books about what to expect or do when you're thrown into grief. I am not a psychologist, and this is not at all that kind of book. It contains personal reflections on my experience; I'm just a person who lived through something hard. If this book provides even a little comfort, vindication, or a pinprick of light for you, I am grateful to keep you company in a tiny way. If my thoughts feel irrelevant or bother you in any way, please do me a huge favor and never read them again, or immediately put the book in your pile of stuff to donate. Just don't burden yourselves with head noise when you have enough to do already (such as the laundry that never, ever ends).

That said, thanks for reading! I would love to hear from you and learn how you can relate to the things I've shared.

—Val
valchangsnekvik@gmail.com
Fall 2018

Chapter One

Trying Out Dating

January 2013

I went on a date this past weekend. It was with Craig, the guy I shared an office with for half a year when I first came back to work after Andrew died. First, let me tell you what greeted me when I entered my office the day I came back to work (a new office so I wouldn't have to work in the one I'd shared with Andrew for six years): a photo of Craig half-naked, eating meat at some outdoor barbecue event.

My first thought was, *What a body!* and my second thought was, *What have these younger punks been up to in my absence?* Unfortunately for my lingering eyes, the more responsible office manager replaced the placards from half-naked Craig a month later and our door went back to purple and gray.

Fast-forward eighteen months and I ran into Craig after he returned from a four-month overseas adventure in Latin America ice-climbing 14,000-foot peaks in Argentina and visiting flamingoes and salt mines in Bolivia. (Yes. Book your flight now.) This moment of intersection as he was visiting mutual friends of ours crossed over with my growing interest in going on a fun date. Voilà! Throw in five minutes of insanity, a sprinkle of carpe diem, and the "you only live once" antidote to neuroticism I gained from staring death in the face, and I emailed him this message:

Hi Craig, Want to go out on a date with me sometime? I know this is kind of out of left field, and you might be leaving the country tomorrow, but I thought it might be fun.

To which my sister who's seven years older said, "ON EMAIL?!" And I'm like, whatever, that is so yesterday's faux pas. The real faux pas are new cultural bridges to cross, especially since there was a noticeable age gap involved in this potential date.

Yes, Craig, my spontaneous date, was a few years younger than me. And as someone who recently crossed the threshold into my forties, it was exhilarating and hilarious at the same time to consider dating someone who didn't wear the tiredness of midlife yet.

Take a walk with me for a moment one summer to Trader Joe's. On one particular shopping trip, I got in a checkout line with a very cute, tall, dark, and handsome Man-Boy who proceeded to ask me what my cultural heritage is. When I answered, "I'm all Chinese," he smiled and asked "Really? Pure? I could've sworn you were mixed." Which I take as a sort-of-racist or sort-of-Asian-preoccupation flirtation. Or maybe it was just a Millennial guy who's in touch with mapping features of all countries of origin. But anyway, the flirtation part got me sort of flustered, and I proceeded to chitchat (with my youngest child standing there staring at the dark-chocolate-covered raisins) about where I was from, where he was from, and totally mixing up Maine geography, much to Man-Boy's confusion. (For your future reference when flirting or just traveling to Maine, Bangor and Bar Harbor are not the same city.) When I left, I swore I would never get in his checkout line again, and on the many visits to TJ's that fall, I furtively looked around the store to be possibly seen by him but never caught seeing.

Oh. My. God. What I learned that day at Trader Joe's is that I am a complete social weirdo when it comes to straight single men. Give me a married male friend and I can banter with the best of them, simply enjoying the natural chemistry of Couples World. After all, I lived in that world for twenty years, and it's all good. But give me a single guy and I'm at an utter loss. I'm either horrified that he might be interested in me or terrified that I might attach myself to him and get rejected.

So I concluded I must get some practice by actually dating. And eHarmony, whose praises I sing for others, was not feeling doable for me at that point. (I did tell you about the 3 a.m. freak-out, didn't I, where I'd filled out the 100-question questionnaire with my friend Louisa in the mountains of New Hampshire and then eHarmony uploaded my answers without my permission and went "live" and suddenly "Shaun from New Hampshire" was in my inbox? Ack! I shut the whole thing down and filled out a customer complaint form.)

Anyway, Craig got back to me. He quoted my line about the date request being out of left field but said he was "down" with it. I translated that to standard English and believed us to be on. Twenty emails later we had our spontaneous date. It was at Christopher's, a pub in north Cambridge I hadn't been to for years and didn't know well enough to have a read on whether or not I would like the lighting.

Despite booking the babysitter early, I was late driving across town, and the radio said there was a twenty-mile backup on the Mass Pike. What the fuck! Twenty miles?! I wouldn't even make it to the pub for another hour. So I started thinking. And being the anal mother of three and compulsive communicator I am, I texted a friend to ask for Craig's phone number. The friend texted back, "He didn't think it was worth it to get a phone while in the country for only three weeks, so the only way to reach him is his email." So stopping between construction cones at Harvard Square, I emailed Craig that I was late. Maybe he'd, um, visit the local library twenty minutes before our scheduled dinner and use the computer there. I then got the brilliant idea that in the old days, we used to call a restaurant and ask a human to look around the lobby and pass a message to someone sitting there, just by, you know, talking to them. So I asked Siri for the pub's number, called, and gave the hostess the message.

Amazingly I crossed town much more quickly than I thought I would, parked (illegally) in the lot across Mass Ave., and met Craig in the entryway of Christopher's. Craig said I might get towed, so I exited, reparked, reentered, and finally sat down to my date. No more avoidance. The moment had come!

And it was fun! Can I first say he was a total gentleman, great fun to talk with, as I guessed he would be, and apparently at ease being on a date? And here's what I learned, if learning was part of the deal for the night: first, a superficial lesson based on a glitch on my part; and second, a more telling gauge of where I was with the whole dating thing. On the glitch front, I made the mistake of starting my vodka-based beverage on an empty stomach. Nerves made me completely ignore the cardinal drinking rule for alcohol lightweights—to eat bread before drinking. After three sips, my face turned purple and my eyes puffy (the Asian lack-of-enzyme issue at work with alcohol), and I began leaning subtly to one side as we talked. I must have looked really weird and sick.

The deeper insight I guess comes throughout the dinner as Craig tossed out a couple of casual flirtatious comments. I realized I was completely out of practice slash inexperienced at flirting. I jumped in about 12.5 seconds after we made a brief toast and said, "So, I hope I didn't freak you out by asking you out. I was just thinking I wanted to go on a fun date, and I thought you're a fun person." And then he smiled and said graciously, "No, no . . . I didn't know you were on the market!" And instead of tossing out a casual, flirtatious comment back, like, "So, what are your tips for being on the market?" (flip hair or something there) or, "Teach me your moves—you've been at this awhile!" or, "What exactly is the 'Chew and Screw' move you referenced on email earlier?" Instead of doing anything breezy like that, I lowered my eyes, probably turned gray (which strangely is the color of red plus purple face) and didn't say anything. Flirty moment killed. Next opportunity for flirting: when I offered to pay and Craig accepted, he said, "This is the first time I've ever let a girl pay for me on a first date." If I were flirty-breezy Val, I could've replied, "Well, this is the first time I've ever paid for a guy!" or, "Well, this is the first time I've ever been on a date!" or if I was feeling a bit more sassy, I could've tossed out, "Well, you're my first, too!" (obliquely referencing sex, of course, but let's not get too ahead of ourselves). Anyway, Val the social moron went completely silent instead, lowering my eyes again (since when did I become an eye-lowering shy girl?!), and the conversational flirty moment was entirely over.

So, in summary: I'm sort of on the market, and sort of not sure. I had fun talking with Craig and felt like myself as long as I forgot I was actually on a date and not just hanging out with a) a girlfriend or b) a married pal. Or even worse, imagining he was c) a friend of Andrew's who was there with his spouse, too, and Andrew and that spouse were just returning separately from the restaurant bathrooms at the end of the meal. No, I was there, single Val, with a single and available man, and there could be flirting involved.

All that said, the date went fine. I survived. My earnest prayers that I wouldn't be totally humiliated were answered (thank you, God!), and except for my purple-faced vodka blunder, I even looked pretty good. The following night I went to a wedding where Craig happened to be also, and I danced for hours with my mom friends, all of whom (along with me) were just wild with delight to be out on the town without our offspring. Some probably had sex that night, but I was happy just to be part of a fun, dressy affair. And I was satisfied for the time being with my girlfriends walking up to me in my secondhand BCBG Max Azria dress and saying, "Val, you look smokin' tonight!"

Here's to practice.

Five Years Earlier...

Chapter Two

When the Shit Hits the Fan

March 2008

"Honey, I've got some blood in my stool. I think I should probably get it checked out."

Two things went through my head, best I can remember that day: first, if Andrew said there was a problem, there was likely a problem since he never made drama about anything unsubstantial. And the second was, *Eeeuw, gross.*

Such was our life, a plain and healthy life of two thirty-somethings with three children. It wasn't really plain: we had jobs we loved that were rarely boring and lived in an awesome neighborhood with terrific friends, so in retrospect it was incredibly easy and blessed. But it was plain in terms of doctors' visits.

"Sure, why not. Just to be safe," I answered.

Andrew went to his doctor, who recommended he see a GI specialist, who told him to get a colonoscopy to see what was happening in his intestines. So he did. I picked him up afterward with the boys that afternoon, and he sleepily made his way to the car with my help and an orderly carrying his jacket in a plastic bag.

That evening, we went out to dinner and found ourselves at the Cheesecake Factory toasting each other: "Thank God that's over!" he said, referring to the humorous ordeal of getting a colonoscopy. They'd found an ulcer, they'd said, and so our evening's conversation centered on my godbrother's teenaged stomach ulcer due to stress and brainstorming ways for Andrew to destress at work. Lesson learned. Move on.

The next day I got a call asking if Andrew was home. "No," I answered. "Who's calling?" It was the GI doctor. "Oh, is this about the colonoscopy results? I'm his wife; I'd be very happy to take the results and give them to him as soon as he comes home." (I knew he was out hiking and praying on a hill somewhere, and I didn't want to bother him in his solitude.)

"No, I'm very sorry," the doctor said. "I can only give them directly to Andrew. Is there any way I can reach him on a cell phone?" I weighed the options. I should have probably known but didn't clue in yet that it was bad news. Again, I was living in the present, interpreting according to my current reality of thinking we lived plain, healthy lives. And the ulcer was surely just a sign of elevated acid in my husband's insides due to work stress. But a doctor's personal call with test results was one worth passing on, if only to bring clarity. So I gave the good doc Andrew's cell number and went on with my housework.

Later, the front door opened and I heard Andrew walk into the kitchen. I met him from the dining room, and as soon as I saw his face, I stopped. "It's cancer," he said. And he broke down in sobs. I embraced him and cried into his chest.

I don't remember when we told the kids. I think it was that afternoon, but I really don't remember that moment. Maybe it's because they were only six, three and one. Or maybe we waited. It was just as likely that we put on a brave face that day and decided to tell them the next. I do remember it was a Tuesday, and we had a ton of people in our house that night, which I think laid out the whole pattern of how we went through the cancer–death journey. These were church people there for a regularly scheduled coaching meeting that Andrew and I led, plus some other friends we wanted to be with that night with the news. People poured out their hearts to us, prayed, lovingly offered practical help, and committed to support us and the boys.

A few things come to mind about the months that followed. Some things have been blocked out of my brain, maybe never to return, or maybe to return later.

One, of course, is the doctors' visits. I have no bias against doctors, had an incredibly positive experience with most of ours, and come from a family of very caring physicians. (I have friends who've had legitimately horrible encounters with doctors, which of course would make cancer that much suckier.) But any way you look at it, it was still overwhelming and scary. We started with a surprisingly big-name Boston surgeon who would do Andrew's surgery. Our initial dilemma was how to approach treatment. Chemo or surgery first? How big was the disease? How far had it spread? How many tests did we want to do up-front, some of which had their own risks, to determine the big "s" word—that is, what stage had the disease reached?

It turns out we had hit the staging lottery—bingo! Of stage 0, I, II, III, or IV, Andrew got the highest number. Colon cancer, stage IV. Unlike test scores where higher is better, however, with cancer, higher means you've got tumors in multiple major organs. So what started off as a mass in his duodenum (stage I) had busted through the cell wall (stage II), invaded his lymph nodes (stage III), and went on a worldwide tour to his lungs and liver (stage IV). So, my otherwise-healthy, handsome thirty-five-year-old husband had a killer of a disease. Colon cancer was reputed to be on the deadlier side of things, and it was already growing maliciously all over his insides. Average life expectancy with treatment? Two years. This statistical average emerged regardless of whether you kept up a steady stream of drugs or punctuated your treatment with breaks to improve your quality of life. And the initial rounds would be hard-hitting, with lots of fatigue and anti-nausea meds to compensate for the poisons being pumped into his body to kill off cancer cells.

So we didn't have much in the way of choice, as far as great outcomes to be expected. Nutritionists and Eastern health-minded authors swore by healthy eating, and Andrew was inclined to try that approach in addition to the traditional Western stuff. So green smoothies and no beer for him. I tried occasionally to join him. But somehow cooking for toddlers and dealing with the whole mess didn't bring out the health nut in me; call me crazy. I ate chips and salsa as often as I ate kale that first year.

What's surprising about shit hitting the fan is that there can be so many rounds of it. The first was the big "C" medical diagnosis. That's like the bucket of water that fills up at water parks and then dumps over everything all at once. But then there are all sorts of squirts that follow. (New England people, I love Canobie Lake Park in New Hampshire, but think Treasure Island with a zillion water guns that fire from four staircases leading to eight waterslides. That's how news seemed to come at us.) One of the shit squirts was the staging news, as I've already explained. Another was the overwhelming nature of online information. I'm not an internet troller or blog reader, and I only got on Facebook recently, so I escaped the excessive ways one can get swallowed by internet content about disease. But it only takes one graph to screw up your day. I found a graph that said there was a 7% chance of survival with stage IV colon cancer. That number, that simple little number children so often use as a lucky number. Once you see that number, you want to read more to find out why that number is on the graph. Does that number represent your spouse? Are there loopholes in the research where people haven't considered that it costs a load of money (like half a billion dollars according to one person I talked with) to prove anything by FDA standards? Maybe there were miracle cures to back up those internet stories about pills and diets and alternative treatments. Surely we'd be the lucky ones, the ones to push that number seven a little higher over time. Or at least, with us living in Boston, the number might be regionally higher (maybe they did the statistical analysis only in rural Philippines—no offense to my Filipino roots).

As we found out over the next eight months, through two surgeries and Andrew's first five-month stint of chemo, after which the cancer reemerged everywhere, there was no miracle cure for us. He tried broccoli and Brazil nuts; he was off beer and meat; he ran a lot in between chemo sessions. He even drank special water that had something to do with removing ions and supposedly had a great effect on some people. (Thank you forever, Rich and Carolyn, for buying us that water in hopes that it might work—you rock.) And because we had heard great stories about the positive effects of prayer, he got a lot of people to pray for him. Like, a lot. And he traveled thousands of miles to go to "houses of prayer" around the country where apparently people had been documented by medical doctors as spontaneously healed. Cool.

However, none of it worked for us. The top of the new year found us in a rut with him facing another round of chemo. This happened right after we found out that my closest friend from college and her husband, who'd started a software company by hiring folks from our church, had been raking their partners and employees over the coals for a decade. As financial wrongs came to light, we found a helpful parallel in the scandal of Bernie Madoff, the financial investor who suckered Jewish communities for millions. Our church had been duped by our own "Madoff," through charming deception and promises that exploited our religious predisposition to trust each other. Worse, I was accused of betraying and abandoning my former friend in her time of need as I sought to protect others who'd been left in the lurch. Later that same year, my coworker resigned with an accusation that I was a racist. There are two sides or more to every story, but let's just say all of that was . . . not fun. I tell you these things not to lick old wounds. I want you to have a taste for how hardship didn't seem to come one drop at a time. It often came, to use my water park analogy, a whole spray at once.

Phil, from my family's grief group, said his whole life in every sphere fell apart during his wife's illness. Even though losing her slowly to cancer was painful and exhausting, losing the company he'd built over decades to mistreatment and cutthroat competition was arguably worse. As Phil put it, he was already spinning with the mess of going through cancer and having a son to raise when the rug was pulled out from under him and his entire identity called into question with his company's failure. It was this loss, even greater than the slow and depressing death of his first wife, that caused him to do major soul-searching and try to emerge ready to live again.

Back to my and Andrew's story, at the center of the spray was, of course, the unfolding reality of his cancer. Try any oft-used descriptions of life dealing with this disease, and it works here: our world was immediately turned upside down with his diagnosis. We had endless doctors' visits and logistics to coordinate, and he had countless stabs and tests. It was mostly unknown but almost always scary. It was also very boring, waiting for results, phone calls, appointments, and rides. Our days were punctuated with the joy of loved ones, especially our innocent children begging to read books on the couch. Friends and family rallying around us made a huge difference.

The bottom line of our circumstances was that we had been thrust into a different life. No one had asked us, and we had no warning (except, I guess, that late-stage red flag in the toilet). Life was, at some level, just happening to us. If you sense passivity in me, you're right. Nothing eroded my confidence in being a 100% active player in my own life than receiving news I didn't imagine, create, want, nor contain, walking alongside a husband who fought and then lost his battle and disappeared, emerging without control of my kids' future or even a full-time job.

Control seemed fundamentally out of reach in my new reality. I'd grown up with a pretty neat existence, in a wealthy suburb with parents who wrote the checks for my glossy higher education. My woes were my woes, and family issues were real. But the generally nice life had been suddenly spat on by our ever-evolving new normal. So, in haste and retrospect, I said goodbye to the tidy life for good.

Chapter Three

The Day Andrew Died

A ndrew died at home at 8:42 a.m. on Thursday, May 20, 2010. But the hospice nurse marked him down as dead at 9-something because they have to make the official time of death whenever the staff member arrives at the house and confirms it. But I know he died the moment I walked out of our bedroom to call down the stairs about the boys, to their grandparents Chuck and Marianne. The reason I know is because he'd been doing his raspy breathing and staring at me as I sobbed, holding his hand at his bedside. And then I told him I'd be back in ten seconds because I had to check on the boys. I walked maybe ten paces to the landing, called down, and walked back into the room and found him gone. Eyes vacant. No more breathing. Not even that sharp intake of breath after a spell of no breath, as the hospice brochure had described. Andrew had had that kind of breath pattern for the last twenty-four hours at least.

Ten seconds, ten paces, and then I was the only person alive in the room. I got up onto the bed and lay with Andrew for about an hour. Later I called the funeral home, who came and wrapped his body and took it away until we buried it the following week. They wanted me to exit the room when they arrived, maybe for discretion's sake. And I said no way; I was going to stay and watch them lift my husband's bony body in its pale green T-shirt and put it into the thick black vinyl bag and zip it up. I guess I felt I owed it to Andrew to keep his body company right then. Then, I followed them down two flights of stairs, whereupon they made the fastest, smoothest, quietest exit from my front door to their vehicle and drove away. Even in the moment, I figured the Brady & Fallon Funeral Service training manual likely included a chapter on dignified departures from the deceased's home. I imagine it spoke of minimizing the trauma for onlooking neighbors, who thought they'd merely stepped out to grab the mail and instead met a body bag holding their neighbor freshly departed.

My first exposure to the Massachusetts General Hospital hospice department elicited a sarcastic laugh. During one of Andrew's oncology visits late in the game, we were sitting in the examination room. Dr. David Ryan had just informed us that indeed the chemo had stopped working, and the radiation to Andrew's brain sucked beans for healing. Radiation preserved function by shrinking tumors, but we were still fucked in terms of any hope for reversal. As if on cue, a nurse entered the room with hospice brochures. Now, if we hated Dr. Ryan or our care up to that point, I'd bitterly describe how lame music also started playing the moment she introduced the topic of palliative care to lessen Andrew's pain while dying. But we loved Dr. Ryan. We loved his demeanor, we loved his explanations, we loved the respect he had afforded us in the two years we'd known him. He was just a guy, it turns out, a forty-something Catholic who probably worked too much and saw a ton of people die. He wore ash on his forehead each first Lenten Day in March (we'd seen the ash streaks twice now), had four kids and spouse at home, and somehow still had a soft heart. David Ryan actually looked sad that day, frustrated he couldn't help more with better experimental smart drugs or a miracle. I believe he also liked us and felt sad that Andrew was going to die. That did help.

Anyway, the brochures. I saw them and inexplicably laughed at the phrase "lessen the pain." The leaflets were varied and multicolored, some with glossy photos of supposedly caring people looking at each other. But like the carpenter's plain cup in the movie Indiana Jones and the Last Crusades, the paper that caught my eye was low-key. A matte pale blue with a simple black ink drawing. The drawing was of a ship, and the title was something poetic like "Gone from My Sight." Under that was the description, "The Dying Experience."

Inside was a road map that would prove an utter sanity pill leading us through the last month of Andrew's life. It was remarkably like a recipe for making cookies. The authors, all hospice nurses, had outlined things in a timeline format starting with one month out. Brief, matter-of-fact descriptions followed each time stamp. For example, it stated that at one month before, a dying person has varied levels of interest in social time. Some days they wish to stay at home and see no visitors, and other days they crave connection with others. Indeed, Andrew fluctuated between asking for friends to join us for dinner or asking me to cancel so-and-so in order for him to sleep for hours.

The peak of Andrew's social output that last month, I recall, was hosting his college best friends who'd come from around the country to bid him farewell. They took turns accompanying him that visit for brief walks around the block, and he sat outside for hours shaking with laughter as they recounted endless dumb shit from the past. The grill and beer flowed without pause. A final group photo had them lined up bare-chested to show off Andrew's skeletal frame next to others' muscle and fat. Even in that last social burst, though, we had grave spells of silence where his eyes hinted of utter darkness. Given the brain radiation screwing with the hair he had left, we spent one morning alone in our shower while I shaved him bald. Well, first I pulled a bunch of tufts out, and then I shaved the rest. He sat rigidly upright, and we didn't talk much. And then he walked downstairs to rejoin his friends.

At three weeks, the brochure predicted, appetite would start to wane. Being a Chinese mother, I was most stressed out by this food-related change. Love equals food-pushing. My formative years were marked by memories of being sick and my mother feeding me some soup or rice and then . . . voilà! Eventually something good resulted as my body embraced that healing nourishment. Not so now, palliative care informed me. Force-feeding a dying patient might result in choking, thus speeding along the very thing a family member hoped to slow down. Comfort was the palliative care folks' highest priority, and food should become less and less important.

Sadly, about three weeks before Andrew died, this prediction played out on schedule. The previous two years of fighting cancer had been the exact opposite, with us trying healthy regimens and Andrew himself standing for hours in the kitchen concocting his latest health cookie or stew. But now, eating actually pissed him off. He'd aspirate regularly, cutting off any enjoyment of flavors or socializing around the table as we all went silent. It turns out that the failure of his tongue function was the kicker that killed him: a huge tumor at the base of his brain had squashed his ability to control his tongue. So sitting up to eat became a sacrificial show of bravery for the boys and me.

Andrew's last notable meal had been his birthday dinner, takeout from JP Seafood Cafe. Our photos, part of the documentation routine at the time, now are glaringly sad. They show Andrew smiling and leaning over to each boy, who stands displaying his hand-made birthday card for the camera. One drawing was adorned with dad and son under a sun and birds flying. Another had thirty-eight candles on a cake spilling out into the margins. Their written messages? Still hopeful for healing and ball-playing. Andrew's smile? Ear to ear, as were his sons'. But ghastly, too, below eyes that carried not only joy but a steely determination to make it through the meal.

Soon thereafter, Andrew went into the hospital one last time. Should I be ashamed I can't recall the exact provocation that last time? All I know is, sometime during the stay, a gazillion people sent messages so that I could read him birthday well-wishes. In the back of my mind, I had also anticipated that Andrew would almost certainly not make it to his thirty-ninth the following year. So, the notes could provide a memorial for the boys to honor their dad, who'd touched a lot of lives. People generously obliged my plea to hit "send" with their sentiments right away and not wait for the perfect edited message that gets forgotten and goes unsent before a man dies. I was eternally grateful for this gift of communal memories to my family.

We returned home May 12 for what would be eight days of hospice. We'd been told it could be a day or a few weeks. A hospice nurse was assigned: Sarah, young and extremely competent. She was warm at our hospital discharge meeting without being maudlin. Her cell phone number went into my flip phone, and I knew her once-a-day scheduled visit was considered standard but carried an invitation to call out for help anytime. We drove home and pulled up alongside the house, same way we'd done for years in bringing home the groceries. But once his feet hit the pavement, Andrew clearly wasn't going to be able to walk up the five porch steps to the front door. His frame teetered, threatening a collapse. Who was with us; Adam, or Chuck and Marianne, most likely? We called the paramedics. Two arrived and carried him chair-style up the porch steps, and then up, up to the third-floor master bedroom. Had I been thinking beyond the immediate task at hand, I would have noted this as the final ascent my husband ever made. His next trip down those stairs would be in the funeral home's black zippered bag.

Lots of equipment goes into the realm of hospice care, like a popcorn machine catalog that includes photos of cotton candy and hot dog warmers. With the bed that enables a raised torso, you can also have a commode, cane, walker, and my metal-tastic favorite, the various medical instruments that surround you at all times. The familiar IV drip stand came home with us, of course, but now we also got a phlegm sucker that was the size and appearance of a 1940s radio. I momentarily wondered if FDR's voice would suddenly start speaking out of it at night. Attached to the box was a coiled cord, and at its end was the actual sucker apparatus, which resembled a dentist's tool. When he started coughing badly, Andrew could reach for the sucker thing, as we ended up calling it. (We did occasionally call the sucker another word that rhymed and started with "f," laughing a bit to ease the bitterness.)

I'd bought sheets before he came home to his new steel bed. They were pale green, twin XL size. Coincidentally, the sheets were pretty much identical in hue to the T-shirt Andrew was wearing when he died. I'm sure we changed his T-shirt daily if not more, but for whatever reason in my head he's wearing pale green for all eight days. I wonder if the boys remember him in any other color? They came to visit him in spurts throughout that last week: before and after school, before and after dinner, before bedtime. But that's what it was—visiting dad at home. So weird. He was always there, which was awesome compared to driving across town endlessly, but he wasn't really home-home. He was now upstairs.

Andrew's waking time lessened, but that didn't preclude him reading a little George R.R. Martin or *The Divine Hours* during the day or sending me increasingly brief emails. I kept these messages for years, even though they were like seven words. They contained requests like, "Honey can you please bring me _____." Sometimes, the phrase would be sent without even completing the request—he would drift off as his finger prematurely hit send from his iPhone 3. The guessing game of how to help him was comical and tragic in its lack of success. The only thing I know for certain that I failed was one night when I myself was drifting off in bed, and an evil laziness came over me as Andrew awoke coughing. I heard him from my stupor, and I imagine I even saw his arm reaching up. And I hesitated to jump out of bed one more time to bring him the damn FDR box. I'll carry that spousal guilt to my grave.

Like a parent whose newborn has colic for six full months or a pregnant woman with 24/7 "morning" sickness, Andrew's relentless hacking felt disturbing, annoying, and inconsiderate. It took over our already-truncated conversations with each other. I knew we were bonded in an utmost dark rite of passage kind of way, but in the moment, it meant a lot of staring at each other half asleep. I sat. I handed him stuff. He handed it back. I ran errands and took care of the boys. I came back and sat some more. I sang to him. We prayed. He walked across the room and back.

Come to think of it, he walked around that room a lot until two days before. He wasn't bed-bound for all eight final days like I pictured he would be, even though days prior he'd been carried upstairs. It might sound like splitting hairs, but since time went so slowly, those six days of getting up spelled many shades of difference. Since he could still sit and stand, we concluded that maybe he'd have longer than we initially thought. Of course, most of the getting up would be to pee, even though he wore Depends. But he also managed to pace around the room, sing-shouting some kind of chant or prayer that sounded like a fight for life. It was guttural and beastly, a primal cry. Though a bit scary, Andrew's marching and noise-making expressed the righteous anger we all felt for him. I was heartbroken that his skeletal frame was bent over even when standing up. But I was ever proud he did not give up his spirit until it was truly time.

T he final descent involved more rites of passage, these ones centered around being a father to his three boys. Romanticizing Andrew and death, many can gush, "That is so amazing," and amazing it was. But it also royally sucked. No one wants to play old patriarch dying in bed with your hands on your son's head to bless him when you're thirty-eight. It's just so fucking wrong. But bless them he did, one by one, on Wednesday morning when we kept them home from school. We'd already had our last family snapshot the afternoon before, which was also the day of Andrew's last poo and the last time he could stand up. Clearly, this was it. The night had been long. Our crazy, goofy faces in our Tuesday pictures just twenty hours earlier belied the grief swelling in our household. But denial serves its good purpose, especially with kids who live moment to moment with hope and love. Wednesday morning, it turned out that the lady we'd hired to take care of Andrew for a few extra hours in addition to Nurse Sarah was a praying lady named Ann who "prayed him up" in loud tones before we took the boys upstairs to be with their dad. Andrew spoke eloquently for several minutes straight—how, I don't know exactly since he'd been nearly silent that morning. Calling out each boy with his unique treasure trove of strengths, he prayed for their growth and life in general. Days later, I wrote down a lame version of his statements to each since he never wrote his words down to begin with. I swear there are too many profound moments to pass on to the boys from their dad, but I'm making sure these words are part of the package they get.

Ann herself had a story begging to be told. She is one of the many strangers who became players in our story, a strong woman who was doing her job but also bringing light into what could have been despair. (Ironically, the official chaplain sent from Mass General hospice department, unlike our nurse and caregiver, brought only negativity into the house. I'm convinced that some people, despite lofty titles, carry with them whatever bizarre dysfunctions they refuse to address. I think there should be something like a metal detector for professionals who go into dying people's homes to make sure they don't drag their own baggage along. Ugh. I was thankful we only had to endure an hour of the chaplain.)

Thanks to the hospice "Gone from My Sight" brochure, I was once again kept apprised of what to expect come Wednesday afternoon and night. Andrew's breathing waxed and waned, his sleeping almost constant. Though he hadn't become delirious as much as he might have, he now exhibited a true lack of lucidity. He drifted, spoke in spurts, then slept. No more coughing, but it was so quiet I longed for the sucker machine to hum again. I had ceased to drop painkiller meds under his tongue since even the tiny amount of liquid would choke him immediately. Sarah had added an IV bag of morphine so that the relief would be constant, increasing, and circumvent his esophagus. Still, the raspy breaths and rise and fall of his chest as he slept told me he was with us.

Evening time, a few more friends came, those faces in dim lighting who held such love and heartache. While they sat with Andrew, I joined the boys to watch a movie downstairs for a spell. Then they said goodnight to their dad and went to their beds. My friend Dana brought his guitar and sang "Here Is Love," which I then continued through the night after he left. The song spoke of eternal things, otherworldly things, things that perhaps Andrew could see more clearly than he saw my face in front of him. Speaking of a God who would usher us in love to an eternal state, the song claimed, "He alone shall be our glory, nothing in this world we see . . . He himself has set us free." I don't know whether the song was spot-on, but that night, it was all I could find to say in the hours past midnight. So I repeated four verses in their endless melodic cycle, trying not to wake him but grateful nevertheless when he awoke and looked at me.

Come dawn, some terrible regrets hit me. I sensed the time of departure was imminent, and gross apology after gross apology came rushing out of my mouth. The sins were old things, bygone things, but things an early death still robs of the sweet redemption old age should bring. Weeping uncontrollably, I could not stop saying sorry for all my failures to him. By my doing so, I think Andrew knew I was letting him go, as well. He'd hung on for just so long and had been a fighter to the end. But his body was quite done. His eyes took in my remorse, and true to his pattern of eighteen years with me, he forgave me once more. That moment I paused to step out of the room to check on our kids, I believe his easy-going companionship was so ingrained that Andrew probably had the thought,

I'll just follow her out of the room to say hi to the boys.

And I wonder still as I thought then, if perhaps Andrew moved forward with me toward the door and then looked back to realize in a flash that he was out of his body.

So quick was that moment, and so irreversible. In the grief group I later joined, one surviving spouse told of waking to find his spouse lying dead beside him. Brain aneurism, no warning. In both cases, a curtain is drawn shut. The birds were still singing their morning song, the same cardinal and tufted titmouse melodies we'd heard for a decade. It didn't feel ironic, it didn't feel beautiful. I just registered everything in the room in a flash, staring at his form surrounded by pale green cloth. Then I called my dad, then hospice, and then summoned Chuck and Marianne to join me bedside. Sarah the nurse came, marked the time, offered brief words and instructions, and left.

Before too long, I brought the boys up to say goodbye. They touched him at my invitation. I wanted closure, especially since my friend G had lost her mother at age four and I felt was left confused, because she never saw the body. The funeral home came, as I described above. I had company from my friend Sandy, too, I think. The boys were with me at different points throughout the day, and the rest is a haze. Hugs. Voice messages. Food deliveries. Mail with notes. Funeral to plan.

No one moment was dominant, but I guess the fact they all really happened is my collective shocking review of that time. Perhaps my weightiest definitive moment came when I collapsed in grief the following spring, on that same carpet spot where the hospice bed had rested, as I finally took off my wedding ring. But the door to my life with Andrew had closed countless times before then, and strangely after that moment, too. Death had come so slowly to us from the horizon, starting that winter day of diagnosis years ago. Then, it did indeed do what it threatened and took Andrew from us. To this day, I can pretty much only agree with my son Mark, who at age three cried out when his dad's coffin was lowered at the burial service:

"NOOOOOO!"

Chapter Four

Why a Good Laugh
Is Always Good

The first Mother's Day after Andrew died, my friend Sandy presented me with a gift in the church parking lot: the book *Bossypants* by comedian Tina Fey. Now normally, I'm not a big reader, which Sandy knew. But at her house a few months prior, I'd guffawed so loudly just reading the jacket cover for *Bossypants* that she purchased the book for me. I proceeded to dig in the minute I got home from church. When my darling offspring asked what I wanted for Mother's Day, I said that I wished to curl up on our living room couch and read this book for a while as they played upstairs, a wish they miraculously obliged. I finished the book within twenty-four hours.

Bossypants is a memoir about Tina's work in comedy, her childhood with its dysfunctions and glorious points, her reflections on entering middle age, and various kinds of relationships. It's at times corny, endearing or impressive; in other words, it's sort of like watching twelve-year-olds interact. Without spoiling too many punch lines for those who may devour it like I did, I'll just say that one of the endorsements on the back cover of *Bossypants* came from trees, saying their sacrifice for the book was "totally worth it." (There's the corn.) When pondering the changes in her life since turning forty, Fey sets you up for an entire chapter of deep insights only to say that the big thing she's learned is that she likes to change her pants after work (which I've found eerily true for me as well). A few quotes from colleague Amy Poehler (another famous Saturday Night Live graduate) provide the more biting insights of the book. Tina Fey is not for everyone, but she struck my funny bone in a big way, especially that Mother's Day.

While I was reading the book, my outbursts of loud laughter periodically traveled upstairs, such that one of the boys would yell down, "Mom, are you okay?" At one point one of them even walked down, looking annoyed, and asked, "Mommm, what's so funny?" not with a curious look, but with the irritated look that kids get when their parent has a grown-up secret. "This woman is just poking fun at how funny life can be," was my response, which seemed to satisfy him.

And that's why, on the first Mother's Day without Andrew there to celebrate with, I managed to actually have a good day. Something about *Bossypants* let me release all the tension, unexpectedly showering relief over the spells of pain.

Rewind to the day just before Andrew died, for example. I went, not knowing it would be his very last afternoon, with my friend Grace to purchase a grave plot for him at Forest Hills Cemetery. She had researched possibilities and had emerged with the summary comparison between two local cemeteries. Mt. Auburn Cemetery in Cambridge apparently equaled Cadillac, and Forest Hills Cemetery in Jamaica Plain, Camry.

We chose the Camry, not only because it fit our flavor a bit more but also because it was so close (one of the boys' regular baseball fields was just a stone's throw away).

Lots of things happened that day that cracked me up, though of course not because anything about the day was funny or lighthearted. First off, as we arrived, the gateway struck me as reminiscent of Disneyland's Haunted Mansion, an exaggerated message in bricks and stones that shouted, "Someone in your life has died!" I don't know why it never occurred to me as strange before, but suddenly it was a surprise that cemetery architecture resembled a cartoon cemetery. (I'm not sure what I was expecting, but maybe something more like Target? Or a gingerbread house? Dunno.) And then, as we parked, I kid you not, the sky turned from partly cloudy to dark and stormy. Rain started coming down at a steady beat, whereas ten minutes earlier I'd left the house in flip-flops. Even though I usually leave the house in flip-flops from May to October, you get the point.

Into the main building we went, only to be greeted by a woman I swear was named something like Tabitha or Millicent. She wore black clothes, spectacles, and a kindly wan smile, and she shuffled around her office in tall black boots. Completing her outfit (I noticed as we exited to take our gravesite tour) was a black umbrella she grabbed from its stand. Outside her skin appeared gray. Did I have acute cabin fever, or was she for real?

We boarded the cemetery van, Tabitha, Grace, and I. She drove us around the historical part first, pointing out the plots of famous people such as poet e.e. cummings (which led me to distractedly ponder how much of my high school literary education I'd ignored and how illiterate I actually was). For a high price, interested families could purchase a plot or two near these VIPs (squeezed between writer Ralph Waldo Emerson and one of the founders of the American Revolution, ladies and gentlemen, we have local lover of mushroom omelets, Andrew Snekvik!).

Sensing my lack of buying power (I can't imagine why, given my glamorous flip-flopped attire), Gray-Skinned Gentlewoman quickly left the more expensive historical section and drove us round to the modern section. Here, she said, were newly created areas for purchase, with lots of availability. There were all kinds of diverse options, too—single plot, double side-by-sides, and bunk bed style (with the nifty description "double deep," which reminded me of scoops of ice cream). The map we'd looked at back in the office included sections such as the "Garden of Everlasting Love," which basically appeared to be an all-Asian neighborhood with great feng shui due to the names and positioning of the stones vis-à-vis the sun. Not quite my style, nor did the cheesy Garden name feel quite like Andrew.

Next section was the "Garden of Meditation." That felt Andrew-y to me, in name at least. We stopped the van and got out. By this time, the temperature had dropped quite a bit and I was shivering even with arms crossed. We strode around and considered Tabitha's next presentation.

"Over here, we have a corner plot along the hedge line . . ." she said, her voice trailing off as she considered my slight frown.

Shuffle, shuffle went her boots over a few feet.

"Then, we have this open area which has very few burial sites purchased still . . ."

"What's over there off to the side, under the row of pine trees? Are those plots for the introverts?" I mused aloud.

Tabitha laughed nervously at my joke and explained that, indeed, there were spaces available under the pine trees. They were at a reduced price compared with other spaces in the main part of the section.

"Plots for sale! You just have to promise not to talk too much," I replied and got slightly awkward smiles from my friend and Tabitha both.

We all stood there with the rain still coming down and me finding myself looking at a small, newly planted tree. It was along an open grassy strip that apparently would remain a grass walkway and only had two plots taken in that exact line. Across the hallway was a plot for a young man who'd died in the late 80s, and a couple spaces down was an older Chinese gentleman, with his wife's name already carved in the stone next to his. A Greek man down the lane rounded out the picture. Nice-sounding bunch.

"We'll take it," I said. One bunk bed plot—single breadth, double deep, with whipped cream and chocolate sauce on top.

What followed was a series of paper signing; pretty quick, actually. One big fat check later, Grace drove me home and I walked upstairs with brochure in hand. I whispered to Andrew something like, "Hey, honey, we bought ourselves some new real estate at Forest Hills today." About seventeen hours later, he died.

By cracking jokes about the experience of plot-buying for my husband, I don't mean to make light of the darkness of that day. In some ways it's more horrible to look back on it the further I get from the week of his physical death. Andrew's suffering was what it was: a terrible case of destruction and unremitting loss that was both unfair and evil. Cancer is always offensive. But something about the fact that life was so terribly wrong at that moment caused me to see how fundamentally ridiculous life can be. And so, even in the face of offensive cancer and death, I found it pretty funny that the woman who sold us the cemetery property wore all black and looked like she'd been living in a tomb for a century or so.

While perhaps I'm a nut case or too irreverent, I find it comforting that apparently others who've gone through (or are still going through) tough times approach suffering with a similar sense of humor. I was driving in Boston today and heard Tom Ashbrook welcome Will Somebody-or-Other onto NPR. In the fall of 2011, Will moved to join the faculty in the filmmaking department at the University in Montana. What felt initially like a leg cramp upon his arrival to town turned out to be an all-organ Strep A infection that caused him to have quadruple amputations, leaving him limbless in a wheelchair for life.

Will was invited onto the radio because at the American Disability Association's big anniversary celebration, he appeared as one of the prime entertainment acts of the event. He has now become a professional comedian, telling funny stories about his loss to audiences both disabled and "normal." He's poked fun at everything related to being a quadriplegic: from the gift of finally breaking his bad habit of biting his nails, to no longer needing to wash his hands after peeing. Will has shared the stage with people who have Asperger's and ADHD and other disabilities, who make fun of their own conditions, as well. Will said that even before turning to comedy as a job, he found humor so helpful in combating depression and processing his loss that his friends were the ones who said he should try pursuing the stage. In the brief interview, Will explained his entrée into comedy with something like this: "It's up to those with these traumatic stories to tell their stories, even with humor, because we're the ones who best understand all facets of the experience."

Hearing that remark on the radio made me burst into tears while driving. Why not poke fun at loss and all its ridiculousness when it helps us let out the tension we hold so much of the time? And why not let other people into our world and our lives by breaking that awkward silence others can feel as they wish to help and fear offending us? I find, as Will seems to have found, that being able to talk and joke about hard things with others creates camaraderie and breeds understanding and support. This is true for me with those who have similar stories to mine but also among friends and family who wish to connect with my story from a different experience.

Sometimes humor goes more or less smoothly for those on the receiving end of it. I remember joking with dear friends shortly after Andrew died that I was considering blowing up a portrait of Andrew to a thirty-by-forty-inch portrait for our entryway, as Chinese people customarily do. The only thing blocking me from doing this was that the practice was typically done for the woman of the home, not the man. So I felt some cultural tension—really, I should put a huge portrait of myself in our house. But that might really mess with my kids: not only did they lose their dad, but now, in addition to having to deal with only their mother every day, they had to stare at a larger-than-life reproduction of her face in the hallway. And that would be really unfortunate, I said, because they already lost their nice parent.

My awesome, loving friends stood there on the soccer field with sympathetic smiles, watching me go off on this. They didn't say anything in response to my joking rant, but oh well. It was funny to me then as it is now. And that's an important piece of the puzzle.

Using elementary school playground logic here, I say if something makes you laugh and it doesn't hurt someone else or yourself, go for it. I don't like treating pain as too sacred, like you have to whisper in its company because it's just so precious. I really don't think Andrew minded when he was sick, as he too would join in with jokes about his terrible constipation or his restrictions on beer drinking or his obsession with making the perfect disgustingly healthy cookie. He'd taste his creations each time and then make the "Eh, it'll work, but let's please not call it dessert" face or the "Gross, I'll try again" face. When laughter between us hinted at tears, we were also pretty quick to shift gears and allow the moment to become whatever it needed to be. So weeping and wailing had their turns at the wheel. Sometimes I think that humor was the best possible onramp to grief: emotions all get intertwined like the ribbons of Aquafresh toothpaste on the old TV commercials. The Grief Experts agree with me, I've found through reading this, that, and the other thing they've written. The Experts with letters after their names, mind you. Well, that's a relief.

Chapter Five

Mothering ITMO

The only way for me to evaluate how motherhood is going is to ask how it's going in the midst of everything messy and beyond my control. And remembering that I'm mothering "in the midst of"—or ITMO, as my friends Will and Kathy call it—helps me enjoy glimmers of good peeping out from mounds of trials.

For example, the first Father's Day after Andrew died, my three sons and I made afternoon plans to see a movie with our friends. First, we visited the cemetery in our neighborhood of Jamaica Plain. Forest Hills Cemetery was nicely close by and homey-feeling, kind of like our Toyota Highlander.

This visit started off like the others had gone. We drove up next to Somebody Papadakis' headstone, turned off the engine, and got out of the car. I opened up the back, and each boy clambered to grab his bunch of Stop 'n' Shop flowers he'd picked out ten minutes earlier. I inwardly cringed at one boy's selection of bright-blue-dyed carnations. But you'll be so proud of me; I bit my tongue. It was all about their freedom and ownership of the moment. Besides, maybe fake ugly flowers were the closest approximation to how surreal our family activity was in the first place; shopping for beautiful things that you then take to a place of death was distasteful anyway.

Snapshot One: Mothering ITMO shopping for appropriate cemetery flowers.

We walked past old Po Chiu Lam's spot, whose wife's name was already carved under his as if she was packing her bag and would be back in ten. And then . . . there he was again. Or rather, there was his rock stuck into the earth, which was over the box that contained his body, which had housed his personhood for thirty-eight years. His $6,000 rock from Norway, with his name etched onto it as if he'd won a pack of personalized pencils at a school fair.

The boys' and my routine was pretty simple. Our structured moment basically consisted of a Colombian tradition we'd learned from our neighborhood florist Daniel, who with his husband Jeb had supplied the memorial service flowers. You remove just the petals from each stem and scatter them atop the gravesite, sometimes in designs. This practice helped because then the boys could each do something instead of just stand there staring at this offensive number on the headstone—this number 2010—which shouted the truncated end of their normal life. I watched them that day, ripping and dropping petals down as they read the headstone aloud. I wondered again what feeling words were going through their minds. That this was sad? Confusing? Fucking insane?

Before I could gather us for a moment of saying or praying something, my oldest, who was eight, decided to hoist a leg onto the flat top of Andrew's headstone. And then there he was, standing on top of it, arms in the air, yelling and whooping. The other two boys looked up mid-petal-dropping (my deliberate son had decided to rip each petal in half, which meant he still had about 1,384 petal drops to go), and they laughed. I couldn't help it; I burst out laughing too. My son on the stone did a little jig and whooped again. I half-worried there were other families visiting lost fathers near us and was afraid of bothering anyone with this loud, absurd scene. I glanced around but thankfully saw no one. So, I did nothing but smirk and surreptitiously grab some of the petals from my five-year-old's hand to speed things up a bit. The dance and whoopfest wound down, and the last petals landed.

Snapshot Two: Mothering ITMO visiting the father's headstone.

Right as we left the spot, the skies erupted in a torrential downpour. My friend Genevieve and I yelled on the phone to each other, calling off our movie plans, not sure we could safely drive to the theater. *Shit*, I thought, hanging up. What to do now that a dark room and lit-up screen, sky-high decibels, and fake buttered popcorn couldn't soothe us this afternoon? "Let's have a home movie night instead," I announced with fake cheer. Weighty groans greeted me back. So head home we did in the storm, with me turning the front door knob slowly upon our return as if a five-second delay would somehow get us through the afternoon okay. Three boys silently trudged across that threshold.

Snapshot Three: Mothering ITMO a downpour and canceled movie plans.

Within twenty minutes, the boys were fighting over which On Demand movie to pick (clearly the mood for *"Brother Bear"* wasn't universal). The decibels increased, and the vocabulary resembled a therapist's list of phrases not to use in a conflict: "You always do this!" and "I never get to do that!" I stayed in the kitchen chopping vegetables with increasing fervor. Finally, I came out of the kitchen to face my children. Unfortunately and very unintentionally, I still had my chef's knife in hand, which I'm sure scared the daylights out of them. I yelled at them about fighting, not helping clean up for movie night, and for bonus threw in the fact that "You WILL have more chores now that Dad isn't here!" All three boys dissolved into racking sobs. I returned to the kitchen, shaking.

My boys lost their nice parent, I couldn't help but think. And now they're stuck with me, yelling at them on their first Father's Day without a father.

And suddenly it hit me, as concretely as my son dancing on top of the gravestone. No one else was going to facilitate the picking of the Father's Day movie. No one else but me could walk back into that living room to comfort them, albeit hopefully this time without a kitchen knife in her hand. And so, nice parent or not, the job was mine to step up. *"Brother Bear"* or another flick it would be, with my help.

Snapshot Four: Mothering ITMO screwing up.

Somehow dinner got put in front of those growing boys. "Sorry," I told them fifty million times, knowing full well that my apology was absolutely essential but was also ancillary. The Father's Day clock mercifully turned to bedtime. And we awoke the next morning having somehow survived the day. I was still my children's mother, and I would step up again on this new day in the midst of everything.

Chapter Six

Survival A Versus Survival B

Mostly written about a year after Andrew died

In a new way, when going through cancer and all manner of other hellacious things (see earlier chapter for a brief recap of what else hit the fan), I gained a new appreciation and respect for just surviving. As I told you, I grew up suburban and stable, so I hadn't known the kind of hardship that my dad had, where a good day for him at age sixteen meant the Communists didn't capture him for their army to defeat another country (or just persecute his own countrymen). Similarly, just to keep perspective, a good day for a female Pakistani teenager might mean you don't get shot in the head for learning to read. But for me, in 70s and 80s Californian suburbia, I had the luxury to always dream big. My bouts of survival were more like, "Will I ever live now that Mom took away my leopard-print bikini?" It gives you some feeling for how I grew up.

But once Andrew was diagnosed, stability and lack of bad news or new trauma were enough to give us pleasure, that special feeling of delight that a day had gone surprisingly well. And through that experience, which included hours of just sitting or filling out forms or coordinating carpools for my husband and my kids, I gained a warm affection for survival. Weird, I know, especially for those worker bees among us who believe in constant vision, goals, and opportunities for growth. But as one of those Type A goal-driven people, I'm a little different now. And I think this is why:

After Andrew died, I wondered if there are two kinds of survival when you're going through a hard time. I'll call them Survival A and Survival B. Survival A is the kind I'll argue you want to avoid, and the kind that made me previously hate anything associated with "just surviving." B, by contrast, is the one I think is worth shooting for when you're down in the dumps, a take on enduring hardship that allows you to emerge with a kind of soft-hearted tenacity. I guess when I say "shooting for" I mean that phrase loosely; survival, to me, intrinsically implies some passivity around setting goals. Maybe survival mode means merely hoping that you don't fall into worse circumstances or trauma than you already have.

Let's first talk about Survival A—the bad kind. This is the totalizing "LIFE SUCKS" sentiment that threatens to overshadow every hard situation and set up shop for good when that situation gets compounded by more bad news over long periods of time. Cancer diagnosis equals trauma. Car accident death equals trauma. Of course, all manner of provocations (not just death) can lead us to proclaim that life sucks: crippling traffic that causes you to miss an interview, a breakup, a bad boss. Survival A adds insult to the "life sucks" initial injury, though. In the days that ensue, the slow, dreadful loss of positive experiences or the continuance of negative ones can gnaw at a person's spirit such that it colors your whole worldview. The Survival A mentality asserts that you're fundamentally alone in the world, and then to top things off suggests that you might not actually make it through whatever it is in any shape worth living.

I remember, for example, wheeling Andrew to the shade of a tree at one of our sons' baseball games late in his decline, very near the end. It was not exactly hot that day, but it was warm enough that the sun beating down through the tree created kind of a humid umbrella (likely made worse by the fact he was a dying man whose bowels were on the fritz, with a little over 100 pounds on his 6'2" frame).

Andrew had brought to the game his smoothie, which was our latest attempt to get something nutritious in him. (I could write a whole booklet on our cooking process over the two years of treatment wherein we tried anticancer foods ranging from cruciferous vegetables to Brazil nuts.) Anyway, by this late point it was rather depressing. His college friends had come across the country to essentially say goodbye, spending time laughing and telling stories and taking walks with him and wheeling him to baseball games. So there we were, with some of them wrestling with my two younger boys and a couple of them standing there awkwardly as Andrew choked out yells in support of our son and between baseball plays took sips of green smoothie.

A moment or two after he took the last sip, he leaned forward in the wheelchair. He gestured with his hand for the bottle, and then, as if in slow motion, bent over its opening and gradually vomited the entire contents right back into the bottle. The drinking had taken an hour from start to finish, but the vomiting lasted long in its own right, probably a full twenty seconds. Disgusting.

The worst part of that moment is that Andrew didn't even have the energy to react. Rather, he sat back in his wheelchair and a minute or two later said something like, "It's kind of hot." So we moved him into the sunshine where the humid tree umbrella wouldn't suffocate him. No one else among us really said anything either. What was there to say?

I hated life at that game. I hated that my awesome husband had to suffer—first by drinking that fucking sludge in the first place because he could barely eat anything else by that point; but second to be seen by others trying in bony determination to feed himself only to vomit it up. I hated that his cheers for our son, while heroic, could probably barely be heard on the field way beyond where my husband was sitting. His voice was throaty, gritty, almost angry as if it knew that its words would do little to encourage a child who couldn't hear them. Thus, nearly negating the monumental effort it had taken to get to Johnson field for the game in the first place. Fuck.

But I also hated life for me. Let's face it—we're all naturally selfish to a degree, and things weren't too enjoyable for me in that moment, either. How come other moms got to sit and chat while dads or second moms got to play catch with younger siblings during the game? What kind of life did I have, standing next to my husband who was wasting away, knowing that my kids were watching their dad slowly die? And the subtleties were hard, too—others not knowing what to say to us but snatching glances or stares. Knowing our neighbors, those stares were lovingly intended, but still. Then there were generous friends or acquaintances offering to help with my boys but others who frowned at my son's angry outbursts on the playground in the weeks things were really hard on his dad. I hated that my old normal life was being robbed again and again. I was sick of being on people's minds all the time. The word "sorry" coming my way got so tiring. I craved small talk and friendly gossip and two-way carpools and two-adult household chores.

Jumping forward to life after Andrew was gone. I recall a run-of-the-mill afternoon at home, where putzing around was the most exciting thing on my mind and having time to do it felt justifiably luxurious. Stephen was maybe all of seven, tiny really when I look back on the incident, and he'd clogged the second-floor toilet with a rather big, um, production. Things rose and flowed over as they do. But perhaps with his magical kid mind doing its magical thing of taking absolutely no responsibility, Stephen walked out of the bathroom and told no one. I discovered this event because, as I stood ready to cook in the kitchen, liquid starting suddenly dripping down from the ceiling. Startled, then worried, I yelled a question about its origin up the stairs only to have my son amble downstairs to inform me of the mishap. He could have been saying, "It's 70 degrees and slightly cloudy," for all the emotion and urgency in his tone. What flew out my mouth in return was a magnitude 8.5 on the Richter scale and included the sentence, "There is actually poo water, liquid shit dropping down onto our heads!" It was the first time I'd sworn in anger related to something the kids had done (wait: fact check me there). I was horrified at how cruel I was. But then again, I was the mom who, instead of pondering a rare slow afternoon in which she might read a book, was rushing to mop up a bathroom floor flooded with liquid poo.

Exhibit A: Survival A.

W hat goes wrong in moments of Survival A is not really just the Big Wrong thing but also the little wrong thing that threatens to cement your identity forever with the Big Wrong. Perhaps it's a play on that saying, "The devil is in the details." Small things, whether positive or negative, serve to create the story of our lives because it's in those details we find sanity or satisfaction, or fail to do so. It reminds me of a recent BBC interview with British social worker Judith Tebbutt, who was kidnapped while on holiday and held captive for ransom for six months. She reflected on-air with interviewer Dan Damon how she spent each day pacing her tiny room and counting steps for hours, as well as slowly driving across favorite spots in the English countryside in her mind. This, to Judith, kept her mind from succumbing to the pirates' control and allowed her to keep her identity while under duress.

After her amazing story of release, which involved losing her husband of thirty years to murder, Judith asserted that she wished not to be identified as an "ex-hostage" but rather as Jude, her nickname among those who know and affirm her pre-ordeal identity. That decision and others like it, she said repeatedly, preserved her mind during and after that whole ordeal. In my interpretation, the decision saved her in part from Survival A mode. Conversely, I wonder if in battling cancer and facing death, small details served up Survival-A style threatened my entire identity. It said something like, "You thought your life was managing okay, but now you are only Val-who-holds-bottle-for-green-vomit." See, the wheelchair ride getting to the ball field in Andrew's last month was actually much harder work, but it had proved bearable. Surprisingly, it was Andrew slowly vomiting at the baseball field that set off my internal "I hate life" sirens. My thoughts in those moments turned to, *He can't even support his son's baseball playing, and the entire community has to know it. We're a spectacle.*

And the afternoon of the toilet overflowing, my realization that another afternoon at home lost to busyness wasn't horrible in theory. But the fact that I am a germophobe and had to clean liquid poo dripping into my kitchen tipped me over the edge. My T-shirt logo that night was Single-mom-who-swears-at-child-while-mopping-pooey-ceiling. I felt abandoned to my worst self. A subtle but profound difference from acknowledging that any given moment involved tremendous difficulty. The moments suddenly defined me.

And so I had some Survival A days in which I felt like there was no god or person who cared enough to make things better. Inside of me in those dark moments, my head and heart concluded that we were utterly alone. I also despaired of making it through with any kind of verve for life. Survival A preached that physical survival was neither appealing nor unappealing. Rather, Survival A implied that I'd likely wake up with a physical heartbeat the next day if someone hadn't murdered me in the middle of the night. Quality of life? It wasn't even part of the conversation. Words to describe me in those moments: numb, dutiful, steeled. One neighbor recently said to me as much when he recalled seeing me run out to the grocery store and back. He kindly commented, "Yeah, I always wondered what was going on for you." Well, Survival A was going on, that's what.

Without beating myself up for whatever I had to go through in cancer or widowhood, I do feel like another approach to hard times feels, well, better. It's what I've already labeled here as Survival B. Basically, it's just noticing and embracing the good that I didn't notice in the other mode. Over a dozen people who gave their weekend so they could paint my fence the week after Andrew died. The friend who rushed over on a scorching day to wrestle my air conditioners into place that first summer. The guy who felt compelled to come sweep our floor one evening. Those college friends who flew across the country to honor my dying husband—their bosom friend—by acknowledging that his life on earth was, in fact, coming to an end. (And who did it in stereotypical Andrew style, with grilling, beer, and lots of roasting each other. Plus Jun, who very uncharacteristically made a photo album of all the guys with captions on every page. Jun made a photo album. One of them said, "Oh my God, Jun made a photo album. Someone must be dying.") My family members whose schedules were torn apart between 2008 and 2010 by constant visits across hundreds and thousands of miles. Dave and Adam and Chuck and others who took on driving Andrew to chemo with me and sitting with him for hours, and others who took my kids out, or left homecooked Ethiopian food on my doorstep (random side note, I really appreciated that yummy introduction to injera and doro wot).

Sometimes, in addition to feeling loved by dozens of people stepping up to care, we had crystallized moments of joy feeling God with us; so we thought then, and so I think now. Maybe it happened as we took a walk in the sunshine, or in a flash of laughter and cuddles with our boys, or even in the intimate conversations between Andrew and me regarding how to prepare for his possible death.

Survival B whispers in the middle of the worst times that you will make it. You're not alone. People care and are weeping and sacrificing with you. And there is a God who's still here with you, fighting on your behalf and inviting you to do the same. The best part about Survival B is that it gives you glimpses of what your life could be like in the future, after the worst of the bad passes. And it won't just be your physical heartbeat that lasts, but also, as Survival B offers, something worth living for.

I had prolonged glimpses into a brighter life when Andrew was still with us, as he was suffering but trying valiantly to camp out in Survival B. We went into the summer of 2009 determined to enjoy the warm months to the fullest. It was a challenging prospect because Andrew had been back on chemo since April. Somehow we'd snuck in a London trip to my sister's after his first round of treatment in 2009 (this was after his break since the previous August). The April travel had started off crazily with the discovery of lice on our eldest son's head. Three shaved heads, two parents prophylactically treated, and twenty loads of laundry later, we'd made it across the Atlantic. Now, heading into summer, we didn't have travel plans in the works, mostly because the hospital kept us on a close leash for weekly treatments and midweek check-ins besides.

What could we do that would celebrate the precious warm, unscheduled days of summer and accommodate such a rigorous hospital schedule? We counted numbers on our calendar with our boys. There were approximately seventy days before the boys returned to school. So we named our summertime the 70 Days of Summer, and we set an agenda with rules: each family member was allowed to pick two things he or she wished to do as a family before the 70 Days were over. Nobody was allowed to edit others' choices except the parents, who could say whether something was impossible and how we could modify it to satisfy the wish. (For example, we couldn't go to the Olympics as our middle son wished since those had taken place the previous year in China. We modified that one and ended up eating dim sum in Chinatown one morning.)

Sam, who was seven, picked "camping" and "Six Flags" amusement park. Stephen, a rising kindergartener, picked "Olympics" and "China," Mark, aged two and a half, picked "parking garage" and "tunnel." Andrew went for a baseball game and bowling. I can't remember what I put.

It was awesome! We took pictures at every stop, including the ninth floor of a parking garage (thanks, Kathy, for that employee pass)! We ran around the Big Dig's new and improved Chinatown water sculptures after consuming delicious dumplings! We camped! We drove through a tunnel! We bowled at Ron's! We saw the Sox play! We laughed at each other. Andrew had ongoing symptoms, the side effects of drugs and cancer, but he was able to be emotionally present for every outing. When the boys and I look back now, I realize that much of our family pattern of decision-making around entertainment follow the happy rhythm of things we put into place that summer. It was a time of togetherness that valued each person and simultaneously called each individual to value others. The 70 Days were tons of FUN. Take that, scary carcinoma!

Even some of our friends who didn't have scary health issues said it inspired them to enjoy life that summer, and they tried their own versions with their own households. What the 70 Days did for our family was to say this: chemo treatments, while invasive on the schedule and on Andrew's energy, weren't going to take more from us than they had to. We weren't going to give in beyond what we had to sacrifice. There was no reason we had to give up what wasn't required of us to lose yet. Why live in fear and worry and despair thinking about what might happen (and did eventually happen) when we still had Andrew there with us, willing to laugh and discover our beloved city with us?

When I think about the days and nights we shared as a family that summer, I am only happy. When I think about the nine days Andrew and I spent in Italy as a second honeymoon that same year, I am only happy. Boy, did we live it up! We drank of life to the fullest, basking in books and gelato and sex and monuments and art. The red wine of Montalcino! The cave-like restaurant where I ordered ribolita stew! And did I mention the gelato? And oh! the glory of an entire estate for us alone (a fluke of the in-between season for rentals), eight acres for a reasonable price all week.

But it wasn't just costly international travel that made Survival B possible. In fact, I wonder if it was the other way around—that a Survival B mentality somehow empowered our adventures to some degree. Enjoying our life and feeling connected to each other and God and friends and family was entirely possible because cancer wasn't allowed to rob us of joy. It couldn't touch our spirits deeper than it had to. There's a verse of scripture that says, "Nothing can separate us from the love of Christ," which echoed through our days abroad and at home that year. Boston local life—the entire 70 Days spent in humble amusements with our kids—was just as sweet and glorious as any travel. Our toddler, whose wish was fulfilled when we parked on the top floor of a parking garage, didn't know the difference between free or expensive wishes. Those simple pleasures of being together with loved ones were a gift that Survival B mentality afforded us, even as Andrew still had to pump drugs into his system and get full body scans and deal with endless side effects of being so sick. Chronic constipation, nausea and exhaustion, neuropathy that caused evermore tingling and pain in his hands and feet, acne in the summer, weight loss, not to mention scary medical reports, all threatened each week to say that joy wasn't worth fighting for. But we did fight for it, and I'm really glad we did.

I think of Italy or the 70 Days of Summer when I consider what a better way to survive might look like, if such a thing is possible. Again, on the worst days of extreme trauma (holding Andrew in his last hours counts as one of these), I have no pushback for numbness. But whenever possible, even when society argues you have the right to be bitter, I say, pick Survival B.

One might argue, "But he died. Andrew didn't make it. So Survival A wins, because here I am with kids on my own." Well, on the one hand, yes. The loss is enormous, the biting sadness ever present in some way. So yes, I can feel defeated when I think of that beloved man not being here to laugh at my foibles today and raise our kids with me. But the time we did have, and the encouragement to really *live* that it sowed into me, made me resolute about pursuing a life that's in full color, even in the face of casualties.

I wonder what Survival B will teach me, the more routine my widowhood reality becomes. I wonder what I will gain by trying to stay open to life and color and connection. I hope it's that I'll get what I need for such a life, and more. I don't want to close myself off into duty or merely a heartbeat. After all, I've tasted of both to some degree and would gladly forego the right to be bitter in order to experience joy and discovery.

Chapter Seven

A Toast to Andrew!

Sometime in 2013

That man was amazing. It's no wonder he gets to be in heaven right now while I'm trying to get warm in this cafe as I type. I don't believe in earning heaven or being good enough for stuff like that, but boy, I can imagine Andrew and God rubbing their full bellies together and comparing notes on great novels just about now.

I go back and cringe when I read my 10th anniversary card to him that was in a drawer of Andrew stuff. (Stuff like the eyeglasses my son remembered to ask for on the day of the funeral so that we'd have them to keep after the burial.) My card to him was so, I don't know, narcissistic. All about me, and how Andrew helped me love myself, and how much I appreciated him putting up with my shit, and how much he helped me get closer to all that's real or true. But still my words just felt so un-Andrew in the way they come across when reread. Andrew was all about asking about others. About focusing on what others wanted to talk about, or ask, or do. Sure, he had his own interests and passions—more about these in a minute. But he came off just so damn unselfish all the time. How did he do that?

There was his roving childhood, for one thing. He grew up in California for a few years and then up and moved to Belgium where he started school as a foreign kid who wore the wrong color socks. Once there, he picked up the language and thrived with his brain power and loving parents at his back, only to move back to the US to land in Florida for a year and then shoot up to start middle school in Maine. He became a Mainer till embarking on college all the way back in California. So maybe through all this, he just grew this enormous love of different kinds of people because he met so many quirky and interesting people in multiple cultures. They say that when you don't belong to one culture, you can adapt to all cultures. (Andrew had a brief meltdown reading the introduction to the book *Third Culture Kid* at one point; he recognized the shared challenges and strengths afforded children of expats in foreign lands around the globe. He certainly came from that stock, as did the offspring of traveling business people, missionaries, military families, and hippies, apparently. His parents camped out somewhere between the hippy and missionary category.) But Andrew didn't just adapt and survive for himself. Somehow, it seems he took all that insight and acceptance of people and chose to actually do good to people with it.

He became best friends with two guys from pretty different backgrounds: Andrew, the Christian kid from Belgium, Florida, and California; Yama the Afghani Muslim; and Kevin the American Jew. They called themselves the "Three Abrahamic Guys." Today that's no big deal (except when it's still a big deal), but in the 80s in Maine, for a blonde American guy not to try to fit in with all the other blonde American guys and instead become a busboy in Yama's Afghani family restaurant is kind of cool. Maybe he felt rejected from all-American culture (he did), but I like the fact that he didn't turn it around and spend all his energy trying to fit back in, which he arguably could have, due to sports and smarts and stereotypical American looks. Thankfully, the guys he gravitated toward also accepted and generously loved him, too.

And Andrew didn't hate American culture, either, which I think is just additionally great. He got to know people on their own merits or jerkiness, or whatever made them tick. By the time I met him in college, he was just the easiest person to be around. It didn't hurt that I found him utterly charming and handsome, complete with cool old orange Volvo perfect for whiling away the hours in. But his flirtatious ways were coupled with the perfect level of depth and conversational ease and that basic level of acceptance of everyone we came across, walking on campus or eating in a restaurant. No waiter or mailman was below Andrew treating them with dignity and respect. No boss or big shot was above Andrew engaging them as a real person with feelings. To see people through Andrew's lens was to get a thrill of every human interaction because of the utter aliveness of it, the potential for humor or insight or healing or simply zest for things he found awesome.

What sorts of things did Andrew find awesome, you might ask? Well, grilling with a cold beer in hand, for one thing. Andrew practically lived for meat on the barbecue out back, in our mud pit of a yard with bare-chested boys running around. Andrew, at some point of every July heat wave, would also be shirtless, periodically leaning back to spread his arms and emit rebel yells of glee. Over time I grew to translate the yells to mean, "I'm just so fucking happy to be alive!" His inspection of the meat's doneness mirrored surgeons bending over cardiac patients with multimillion-dollar instruments. Additionally, there was the poet in Andrew who searched and searched for words to express whatever feelings he was having, with an artist's soul that his friend Joel called "The Meaning Millionaire." Often Andrew's quest for expressing the meaning of a moment happened to his own frustration, whether because of his mild dyslexia or his bilingual roots. If only sex could speak instead of English, because Andrew dripped with passion for everything from actual sex to a pot of chili to the worlds of *Endymion*. It's a good thing that words and his ESL-like struggle to express himself in the moment did not have the last laugh. All I had to do was look over at his hands, formed into pursed pointers, and I would know the joy, or the anger, or the complex swirl of insight he was experiencing. Hand motions and a range of smiles were Andrew's best tools to get a point across, as well as those caveman yells, at times.

Speaking again of those yells, there was the campfire with Jun and others in Arizona when we were dating—oh God, in 1993. It's embarrassing to remember how much drama we had on that backpacking trip. But Andrew was incredible one night, letting out all his anger toward life and women in general (or maybe just his crazy girlfriend, come to think of it) as he basically chopped down an entire tree and threw it branch by branch into the fire. That fire got pretty big. I remember looking out of our tent to see his face glowing above the flames as his arms waved in big circles, ripping branches apart and throwing wood down. I could be imagining this next part, but I think his hair was even standing on end. The next morning, in the gray light of dawn with instant oatmeal in our bowls, Andrew calmly said his piece in English. While words helped some, I think he'd already gotten his deeper point across, and I apologized. Amazingly, in our marriage, that kind of occasional fireworks display of emotion never seemed directed right at me in rage but rather somehow meant to communicate his strong feelings in a way that drew me in with appreciation.

M any years later, Andrew stood up to the test when he heard accounts of those wronged in our church community by "Madoff," whom Andrew also nicknamed "the Wolf." Among our church staff, Andrew was the first to wake up and realize that this couple, whom we'd all thought were wonderful, were not in fact that wonderful. Andrew led meetings with this couple in an earnest attempt to help them see the error of their ways, pay people back, and get reconciled with others. When all hell broke loose and eight months of the Wolf running circles around us ensued, Andrew stayed the course of justice and supported the rest of us joining the front lines of confrontation. Andrew never once spoke with casual spite or mocking toward them, though. Despite his personal sacrifice to engage in the process (he was back on chemo with worsening side effects—it was 2009), he focused on protecting other people and offering a fair process to all parties.

Andrew going through cancer was just overall amazing, too, in its utter lack of drama. Many who suffer wax eloquent, mourning to any who will listen. But Andrew's handsome ways included not saying much (except for occasional email updates), only doing whatever was in front of him to do. He did this day after day after day. And he did it with grace. Even when his head hung in pain or exhaustion during treatment, he used what energy he had to lift it and smile at whomever was speaking. That speaker was often one of his sons, fresh from a round of tag in the yard and wanting dad to watch them pull a worm from the ground mid-tag. Or he'd use his energy to put hands on a shovel, slowly and deliberately lifting clods of dirt out of the earth so that we as a family could bury our dead lizard and honor its life. What fitting beauty that, to bury Andrew, hundreds quietly filled our church to say goodbye and honor his life of grace.

Within a year of moving to Boston, Andrew was asked twice by new friends to stand with them in their wedding as a groomsman. At the time this didn't surprise me, but later when I looked back, I realized that I didn't know anyone else who'd had that experience. When Andrew traveled to a week-long conference one year, he got invitations from the team putting on the conference to join their teaching team for future conferences. When he officiated a wedding, both families of the couple fell in love with this guy who embodied laughter and wisdom, warm affection and intellectual capacity all in one. That was his magical way with the many lives he touched.

Just before he died, Andrew remembered his mother's pain in her loss of another child when Andrew had been a mere four years old. "It's not fair," he told Marianne about the car accident death of his older sister Amy, and now his own imminent departure. The way Andrew cared for and honored his parents during his own terrible suffering was also exemplary. He also extended a generous offer to me, partly in humor when we sat in late-night conversation, and then later in earnest when it was clear he was dying. "You should definitely marry again," he told me with twinkles and tears in his eyes. "I release you to do it," he added with uncharacteristic formality. This, in the middle of him needing help to go to the bathroom, thinking of my welfare and happiness.

I wish, I wish, I wish I could know you more, Andrew, until the old age we planned on. I wish I could share with you the pride and worries about our boys at the end of each day as we used to. I wish you would tell me what you think of my trying to write a book about us, and you, and life, crying here in Caffè Aromi. I wish you would grill for us again.

Thank you for being book-worthy, for offering yourself to me in such a profound way, in part because we didn't dwell on the profundity of sharing life with someone. The things I miss most are, of course, what those who've lost someone always say. They are the little ways your face changed with a passing thought, or the parade of condiments you pulled from the fridge before taking your first bite of my dinner. The annoyances that I fought for so long are long gone. What remains is the utter human glory of you.

Thank you, thank you.

Chapter Eight

Anger Interlude

Sometime in 2013

I got so fucking mad this week.

I'm wondering if my grief has been delayed years, possibly even since Andrew's initial diagnosis. Maybe I stuffed everything into a bag because I had to put on a brave face for the boys. Maybe, as my friend Kathy says, I ended up taking care of others who were also taking care of me.

Or maybe I've just spent down whatever resources I had going into cancer, and I was lucky enough to have five years of grace piled up in me. Andrew and I often wondered aloud as people praised "the way you guys are dealing" with suffering because we had generally good attitudes day-to-day. On the one hand, those statements felt intrusive to us, as if we were performing for watchful, evaluative eyes. On the other, we were glad that our hopeful attitude was making a positive impression on other people who might feel encouraged to face their own bag of troubles (rather than, I guess, had we chosen to "curse God and die," as Job's infamous wife suggested in antiquity).

Having five years of resources to spend down is pretty damn lucky. I realize that not everyone is so blessed to have that going into cancer/disaster/death/grief. But I had a great husband, a devoted family, and several loving communities around me when I first entered crisis. Can't take any one of those things for granted. People sent us money. I was greeted with Edible Arrangements fruit bouquets for our family on chemo days. I had a job I generally liked. I had a dad who'd lost both parents in World War II and survived and thrived with a hopeful spirit.

Most significantly, to me at least, I had a storehouse of years where my experience of connecting with God felt relevant to facing difficulty. I didn't believe in a God who promised a life of first-world-only problems (as I've thought a million times, the Bible was all written during the general mayhem known as f'ed-up world history). So I felt like I knew a Someone who had seen the world suffer through millennia of troubles that included the atrocities of war, poverty, and the craziness of disease, not unlike cancer today. So, I didn't ask the inevitable "why me" questions of suffering. I didn't feel particularly alone, knowing that many people, including twenty-somethings today, lose their spouses and are left to raise children alone.

But this fall, I hit some bumps in my insurance, which had until then gone pretty well with Massachusetts state-sponsored help. My kids and I were all kicked off our medical plans, which in the end we probably didn't qualify for, given that the boys' survivor benefits plus my part-time income put us just over the income bracket to get real help. Within a few months,

I was then sent multiple confusing letters rerouting the boys' care more than once and putting them on plans that apparently had no emergency coverage. I myself had to purchase individual coverage for dental and medical, totaling $360 per month just for me, since my longtime job didn't provide benefits for part-time staff. (Things have changed since then, and my new eligibility status made for a happy chapter ending—thanks, workplace decision-makers!) When I investigated the options for supplementing the kids' state-sponsored routine care package to include things like stitches in the ER (for a boy falling off a tree limb he was climbing, just hypothetically speaking), the man on the phone told me that the supplementary option was only available to people with less than five years of immigration status. Well, I love a provision specified for recently immigrated folks, but no opportunity even to have ER coverage for added fees? *No*, phone man said in the most bored tone ever. This was after he cut off my one-sentence description about my single-parent situation with, "Well, let's stick to the important information." Have a five-second heart, you asshole.

So, I looked into private rate family plans and considered just sucking it up and opting out of any subsidized insurance to pay for solid coverage. Bam—$770 per month. (That was over half each of my paychecks.) But here's the catch. Even if I said, "What the hell, I'll pay cash and we'll eat all rice and beans, or just rice, and thank God I have a small mortgage," I still couldn't do it. The open enrollment for adding the kids to my plan wasn't until July. So I was stuck for a few months hoping my kids didn't break a bone, or get more than a cold, or something even worse.

So, there was the insurance issue. But that's just one of the things I could bitch about. The single-parenting thing, for another, was getting to me. The cumulative effect of having no relief parent at the end of the day was bugging me more than it had for the first couple of years. And now that it's hitting me, it's hitting loud and clear:

My tank is flashing red on empty.

My friend Gayll, who was coming through Boston this week (of all weeks, the one of the 2013 Boston Marathon and its horrible bombings), said something wonderful to me. I was relaying the "Mommy is losing it" incident from the car during my family's getaway to a friend's house in Cape Cod. The one where I yelled at the near-top of my lungs how fed up I was with my kids' ingratitude for what they had. The one where I quantified how many trips to the recycling bin it would cost my one son to pay from his chore money for his soda and dessert from the restaurant (the $80 lunch he'd just called "cheap" and "a good deal.") ("Someone has to work for that $80!" I'd screamed.) The yelling bout where I quantified how many loads of laundry or rounds of trash-emptying my other sons would have to do to pay. The one where I vented that I might want to work full-time to get away from being with my kids so much. (Yes, I did say that. Ouch.)

Gayll looked at me lovingly as I shoveled mouthfuls of beef jap chae into my mouth at my favorite neighborhood Korean-Japanese eatery. Food therapy never tasted so good.

She asked me, "What do you need?"

And I said, "I think I need more love."

And she said, "Maybe not just for the kids. Maybe for you, too. What would you do if you had more time for yourself?"

And instantly, I thought of this, like the voice of God coming up from my beef dish and out again from my vocal chords: I WOULD GO TO IKEA.

Gayll laughed and asked, "Really?" (Like she didn't know her friend was so materialistic. What about nature walks in a New England springtime? Nah, just bring me the Swedish meatballs and cute, cheap curtains.)

"Really," I said. "Because I've been fantasizing about getting curtains for my bedroom for a long time."

"How long?" she asked.

I thought about it. I assumed my answer would be, "since 2008 when Andrew was diagnosed." But what came out of my mouth was actually 2004. Yes, that was true. The year my second child Stephen was born, Andrew and I had moved our bedroom upstairs because he'd noticed it was the biggest room in the house and we were the grownups, after all. Okay, I'd agreed. I'd meant to buy curtains, but life was busy with two toddlers. Two years later we had another kid and entered the parenting world of three-on-two. And then two years after that, Andrew went into cancer treatment, and two years after that, he died, and three years after that, I was sitting in JP Seafood Cafe with Gayll eating beef jap chae, still with no bedroom curtains.

"You should really get to IKEA," she said. "I'm going to text you on Monday when I'm already gone from Boston."

"Okay," I said.

So, I wonder if IKEA will get me what I want. Will it make me a nicer mom? Will it make my skin crawl less when I hear the boys fighting? Will it make me soften toward my kids when they are ungrateful for a restaurant meal? Will it help me accept my in-laws' quirks better and give me more energy to call the insurance lady back? I don't know. I guess I'm thankful to think that maybe God and the universe aren't out just to make me a slave. It's nice to think that beauty and fun and pleasure aren't gone from my life, and that in addition to budgeting our family's meals I could budget money for house gadgets that I like.

But in the end, I also think that I need something more. I had a good cry this morning that makes me think there's some further release needed. This release is about anger toward Andrew, and bewilderment and distrust toward God, and truth-telling about my own state of being. I vented in my journal the other day, basically a kind of "Fuck everybody" sentiment, for leaving me to raise my kids on my own. It really hits home when you're three years in, in a way that it didn't for me in the first two years or the two after diagnosis. The initial grief was shocking and offensive; death can deal a pretty harsh blow to a family. But over time, the dull ugliness of a hole in the family picture feels just as bad, if not worse. The fact that the baseball schedule for three boys means I'm either on the field seven times a week (between 1-3 hours each time) or my kid doesn't have a parent there with him. The fact that the dirty socks (yes, it's a cliché, but clichés exist for a reason) don't get picked up unless I do it or remind others for the umpteenth time. The fact that my body is so horny and yet I'm getting counsel from well-intended friends not to give the impression that I'm too easy on a first date. If only I were facing any dating problem close to that! Instead, I am repulsed by awkward men who seem interested in me in a passive sort of way, and curious about men who appeal to me but are too appealing/young/taken. And it pisses me off that I was at the statistical height for women's libido (thirty-five years) when Andrew was diagnosed and we were fully enjoying our love life, and then he was sleeping with the fucking tubes in his arms and a beeping chemo machine for days on end. And then he was in a different bed with the horrid phlegm sucker in his mouth. And then he was gone.

I don't think I've been in complete denial of grief, since kids and their unrelenting needs 24/7 slam me with loss's concrete reality. But a certain aspect of my denial stage has had a longer life than I'd thought. Maybe part of what I'm realizing in fuller measure is that the kind of life I wanted, that "peaceful, happy life" I once believed an okay thing to wish, wasn't meant to be for me, at least on the terms I once thought. A meaningful life, hell yes. An influential life, perhaps so, in my small way. But the life I wanted since I was a kid, a life where I was essentially simply happy—well, that aspect is partly stolen by cancer and death.

Maybe that "happy life" I held up was fine in some way to wish for, but maybe in another way, it was a kind of Oscar-y fairytale idol higher than everything else. My dad used to speak sarcastically of his secretary who made 50K in the 80s, saying "She has a good salary, and she's happy. She's . . . happy." What he meant by that was, I should aspire to more than simple happiness, because his secretary could have done more with her life but didn't. I loathed his comments in my teenaged brain and spat back in my own head, "I'd love that life. I'd be happy with that life. Screw your ambition." So when I got meaningful work and purpose in addition to a great husband and healthy kids and a beautiful city, even better. But my mind has wandered back to Dad's comments since Andrew's sickness hit, when my simple, blessed life came to an end. What if Dad was right in some twisted way? Not in the way that judges people who don't become CEO's, but in a way that meant he sensed something in that colleague of his that was less than her own possible path in life, a path that could've been more than a stable salary. Again, it's not that I agree with his tone based on what I know of her (his secretary always seemed nice to me, anyway), and I feel bad that he seemed pompous at times. But in a weird way, I'm actually engaging that issue, which is the question about my priorities. What if happiness for me will be a bit more complex than it used to be? What if feeling good and looking good and generally enjoying good circumstances is just not my deal? What will I do in life to live whatever life I could live, to bring the most possible good to others and the most fulfillment and peace and yes, happiness, to myself—ultimately?

I don't know what all this bullshit philosophy amounts to, but there might be something there. I have to chew on it more.

Chapter Nine

Dating Diary

January 2014

I finally gave in to the 21st century idea of online dating. Actually, that's not quite true. As I mentioned before, I very briefly engaged the subject in 2011 in the mountains of New Hampshire. That first foray lasted about four hours total. Then this past year I filled out an eHarmony questionnaire only to see my answers stump the software, prompting eHarmony to erase my questionnaire and suggest I start over, "making sure I have enough sleep, and that I answer all questions honestly." Well, stupid dating website, who died and made you matchmaker god? I guess the ways I described myself and the things I put for my "requirements" in a match outstripped the algorithm they use in terms of allowing for complexity. Sheesh. What an ordeal. Once again, I took my already-private self and decided—not for me.

Then came a frighteningly pointed conversation with G and N at a lunch that was meant to celebrate their birthdays. The reason I say it was meant to be for them is that I ruined the party by collapsing into tears when N cornered me on the dating thing. She didn't go so far as to say, as she did two years ago, that I just might need a dick in me as soon as possible. To be fair to my amazing friend, she wasn't ever far off from where my mind had often wandered. My sex drive was alive and well, and I had already embarrassed myself by foisting my crushes on people who were either a) freshly divorced or b) newly married, oops, move on. But as we left our lunch that day, N's directness touched a nerve. I burst out, "Do you have anyone to actually march in front of me? Like, a real person? It's not that easy!"

And not easy is true. I did start corresponding with people on OKCupid after taking the plunge with two friends-in-questionnaire-filling-out-crime, yet again. I accomplished this, I'm proud to say, right under my own roof with the boys upstairs getting ready for bed. I had an answer for them all ready in case one wandered down while we poured wine and busted out the dating-is-stressful chocolate stash. "We're working on Steph's work questionnaire," I was ready to say. Thankfully, no interruptions occurred, and we had the couch all to ourselves in quiet. I will introduce the boys to Someone someday, hopefully, but not yet.

This time around, after registering my information I actually read the profiles of the 27 men who appeared as potential matches. First, let's just say that being solicited for deep massage by someone who describes himself as "Hot . . . and Safe" and posts his bare chest as his profile photo isn't my cup of tea. There's been about a million examples of this kind of initial contact. Two days ago, for example, I picked up a message from "So Krispy . . . So Krispy" and promptly deleted. (Random question: Why do people with icky usernames use triple dots in their titles? Is that to soften the effect of coming off gross? Again, not . . . my . . . cup of tea.)

So, after deleting a lot of back massages, which despite my aching back I wasn't tempted to follow up on, I happened upon a human-sounding man a few days ago. He lives in Brookline, is a secular Jew, and had about ten poetic things to say, ten emotionally intelligent things to say, four musings about online dating, and a few other details, including patterns of his past love life. I was intrigued. First off, I was intrigued because this was definitely not a Man-Boy. He was experienced, as he described it, with having loved and lost and also been loved and been lost. I liked his forthrightness that came across as neither sappy nor mechanical.

The fact that this person was in touch with his heart didn't mean that his intellect didn't intimidate me. Education? PhD graduate. Whether that means he's a barista and spinning poetry while filling latte orders or works at a university or is a Nobel Prize winner, who knows. But even though I'm smart, I'm not easily comfortable with a conversation that makes me feel like I have to be smart. I'm not that smart.

On top of that fear of hyper-smartness, I noticed that he describes himself as "Agnostic and very serious about it." Given that he's forty-seven, a scientist and clearly also a composer, historian, and all-around very intentional, forthright person, this is clearly a statement about something that's important to him. Hmm. What does that mean to a person who's Christian-background but sick of the American brand of Christianity, liberal in almost all politics, connected personally to the Person I picture as Jesus-God, close friends with people of all stripes gay, straight, Jewish, Buddhist, Muslim, Christian, spiritual, secular, and looking for love? I have no idea!

So, of course, given all that ambiguity on intellect and personal beliefs, I reach out to say hello. Duh. I'm seeing a pattern in my responses to fears. Dive blindly right in? Often, yep. I don't think of myself as always jumping into my fears and initiating with men. But if my paltry dating experience in the past is any indication, I guess I do jump in. There was Mike the football player, a junior at my high school who'd just broken up with an older cheerleader when I, a freshman with a crush on him, was not bothered at all to ask him to our dance. He broke the bad news to me while I twirled the phone cord at my kitchen counter: he and she were kind of back together, but he was really flattered I asked. Then we talked for half an hour about the ridiculousness of some of our German class assignments, the class we shared. Aw, just thinking about Mike makes me think fondly of that guy all these years later. But that's sometimes the curse of being a "strong woman." We just might not get a lot of invitations.

The message I sent Mr. Brookline (my first "first message" online) was something like, "Tell me who's your favorite composer" in classical music, clearly a love of his. And "What's a favorite twist of history you've enjoyed thinking about?", also a self-professed interest on his profile. Both are also genuine interests for me, so I'm curious what he'll say.

He writes back answering both of those questions, not surprisingly thoughtful, in a nice, fun sort of way. Then he asks what I do for public speaking. Then he hits head-on the potential conflict of interests we might have with him as a serious agnostic and me looking for someone who might be spiritually compatible. He confesses he's not anti-religious but is also quietly skeptical of humankind.

While all the actual things he says about his world view are fine in my book, the focus with which he says them is unnerving. Is this just maturity coming through on the internet, where a man who really knows himself and is smart (again, that smart thing coming through) is able to pretty precisely articulate what might come up as a challenge for a serious relationship down the road? That's quite different from the tact other men have used in being friendly and superficial to a fault (like the guy who picked up on my interest in the Celtics and wrote me, "I just moved here. Go Bulls." Or the Greek guy who quipped, "So you all set for this snowstorm tomorrow?" Um, yes, Mr. Greek guy, I have a shovel and milk in the fridge. I'm good.) Mr. Brookline is right to highlight this important issue, but then who knows what would happen? I basically answer him as much. I don't mean to sound glib, I write, but I think it depends on what kind of agnosticism or what kind of faith a person practices. It's clear to me, I agree, that for two people looking for intimacy this difference could become a roadblock instead of the other way around. And then true to my British roots, I sign off, "Cheers, Val" as though breezily pouring lemonade without a care in the world whether he decides to reject me or not.

That was ten o'clock last night. And I haven't checked my messages today, as I'm trying to only do that once a day.

I'm fighting the fear that if he gets back to me with a no thanks, I'll crawl, red-faced, back into my box that is labeled "I'll Never Find Anyone Who Gets Me." I can't help but pine internally, thinking, Andrew got me. Andrew got me in every way you can get somebody—intellect, body, soul, and spirit.

Well, at least I've got that wind at my back. The memories of past love do buoy my spirits, and the fact that it was so incredibly blessed helps me believe I could find another partner who is balanced in the way of mind and spirit, body and soul.

Mr. Brookline may, or most likely may not, be the person for me, but at least I'm interacting with someone to figure that out. And I have to say, it's nice to have a single man ask me what my story with classical piano was, a talent that's truly lived in the closet for most of my adult life. And even discussing what might or might not work in a relationship feels kind of exciting, since I'm having that discussion, however briefly it'll prove to be, with someone who's also looking for a relationship. Taking these things out of the realm of fantasy and coming into the adult realm of figuring things out feels healthy.

So despite my knee jerk reaction to my friend N and her suggestion about my immediately needing sex, I have to admit that she's right to point me in the direction of real, live people sooner rather than later. She knows I live in my head and often get tangled up in imagined failures. Thanks for loving me, N. Glad I'm still a woman to you.

April 2014

I made a really fancy Easter dinner last week. In part, it was all I could do to manage my hormones after going out on a date with D, a European who grew up in the States. He was sort of lodged in my head even though our date consisted of me wondering if he was slightly or more than slightly depressed. When it took him awhile to talk, I resisted the urge to play counselor and instead let the silence hang there. It wasn't all that bad since he was more handsome than his online picture showed and his eyes were nice to look at. Afterward, I'd emailed my sisters and girlfriends with a report: it was a 5 out of 10. It wasn't as if he'd yammered on about himself all that much; it was just that he didn't peer deep into my eyes and ask me what my biggest dream in life was and how he might play a part in my getting there. Fantasy killed. Enter: real person, who'd divorced his wife eight years ago, reengaged to a degree when she was diagnosed with breast cancer, raised their many kids after she died, and works in software engineering and had a promising product tank last year in reviews.

All that said, this real person intrigues me. He asked at the end of our lunch if I'd like to meet up again sometime. "Sure," I said. Would I like to again discuss Communism, teen suicides in Massachusetts, immigration, religious baggage, parenting as an only parent, and inventing new electronic instruments? Why not?

The strange thing is, this one meet-up with D is making me think that someone whose daily life more closely approximates mine would be a great catch. Most online people seem like an advertisement for REI or Forbes magazine—so damn sparkling, with more promise besides. Active people looking for active women, women who can hike, have a career, produce kids at some point or raise his, laugh their way through live comedy shows, hold fascinating conversation, look really hot, and go to music concerts at cool small venues to discover future talent together. That, or just support a man whose real passion in life is cheering the Bruins in a bar. I'm looking for someone who wouldn't mind me actually being me, in all my boringness or interestingness. Saddled with responsibilities but constantly pondering the possibility of new things. Devoted to parenting, but not so consumed with parenting that conversation must always drift toward the amazing or terrible things your kids did every moment of the day. Something about the middleness of D's midlifeness struck me. He, seemingly like me, has about 90% of his time and energy spoken for, between having work meetings and going biking with his daughter, or fixing a fence in the cold over the weekend. But it hasn't killed his philosophical bent, or the fact that talking about his Communist grandfather is the story he likes to open his dates with.

Our next meet-up is set for next week. We're going to walk around the waterfront if the weather is nice. I'm nervous and think the time in between date #1 and #2 is a bit long for my taste—two weeks. But that's the way it had to be since our kids are on school vacation this week and I don't feel quite ready to see anyone in the evening. He's texted a few times, brief things, like the bit about his fence or going to the Cambridge Science Festival with his kids. I've liked it. But I don't want to build a life with D, a near-stranger, in my head in the meantime. Maybe he has no friends and little emotional intelligence. Maybe his business ventures have changed so often because deep down he's an unstable sociopath, just like my former friend's husband. Or it might end up that he is stuck in grief and loss, or has too dark a personality for my tastes after all. Or maybe he'll decide, if he hasn't already, that I'm the one who's too [fill in the blank] for him, or the timing's just not right.

Either way, I suppose this is how life rolls with dating in widowhood. I guess I'd better walk up those stairs to fully board the bus, because it seems to be moving.

After Date #3

I've pondered the idea that D put a bug in my home when he picked me up for our last date. It occurred to me the other day that I'd left him alone downstairs while I went upstairs to the bathroom before our walk in the Arboretum. I think about strange and nefarious things people do in movies that involve invading innocents' privacy. Since I've actually known dangerous people who cheat their way to favor, the idea that D might have come to my house with evil motives lingered longer than most aberrant, disturbing thoughts. Funny how entertaining negative thoughts can take on a life of their own—like wondering if he was listening to me playing piano this morning and wondering too if he knew I was thinking sadly about our dates while I did it.

I think my fear and musings about D installing a listening device that day are my strange way of coping with the lack of ongoing communication with him. It's been five weeks since we met, and we've exchanged a couple dozen texts in and around four dates. The last one (twelve days ago, but who's counting) was right before I left for my work conference). Since that trip, he texted me, "Hope you had a great trip," after which he informed me his oldest daughter was returning home and that he was scared. Since Friday night (it's Tuesday afternoon at 4:15, but who's keeping track), I haven't heard from him. He told me things were going smoothly. She's had issues since her mother died and has been at boarding school.

So understandably, between that daughter and his four other children needing his attention, he might be a little unavailable. But it's so hard not knowing.

It was rosier when we went for the walk that day in the Arboretum, as lilacs were still budding and the dogwoods lying beautifully fully flat on their leaf plates. Crabapples, often the lesser cousin to real apple trees in my former life, bloomed so magnificently that D said, "We should come here every week to see them." He'd said other things that day, tender or romantic things, but I wasn't sure enough how I felt about him yet to answer definitively back. I hope by now I've made clear that my affections have been growing. But that day, it was nice that he reached back to offer his hand as we climbed down a mild slope. I was shy to take hold of his hand, but I noticed and liked it inside. The best part of that outing was his embrace when we said goodbye. It's an embrace I hope to repeat or build on—and this is the wistful part of recounting that moment. He pulled me in and placed his right hand at the small of my back on the right side. If I pause here, I can still feel the warmth his hand emitted, and likely my body radiated from that spot as he did it.

It's been so long since I've been embraced like that. Tender, with just the right amount of sensuality of two adults getting to know each other. Two people who've been through a lot and still carry tons of only-parent responsibility. He has been divorced ten years and has been with several women (three he tells me, who were close enough to bring home to meet the kids). But three women in ten years means in my mind that he's not a player. And I could tell he is also serious, tentative, and focused about what he's looking for.

Which makes the silence all the more meaningful now. He's shown himself over the last five weeks (seven if you count our correspondence online) to be consistent and straightforward. I wish I wasn't so closely focused on the time, the day, the silence. But I am. So I sit here and wait.

Wednesday

Torture. One text last night and none today means I'm stuck in a perpetual cycle of torture. Ugh.

Tuesday

I hate to say it, but maybe my friend Will is right. Before my next date with D, I stopped by to see Will since he hasn't been on my SOS email updates to girlfriends. Will, just like Andrew was in some ways, is the best straight-guy girlfriend around. He's so in touch that his wife thought he was gay before they hooked up. Anyway, Will said lots of men end up emotionally comatose by the time they're forty (or way before, warned my friend Arianne). "And so," Will said pointedly, "you gotta move on, fast. They will not change." He'd learned from dating women that even if he felt there was potential, basic personality change simply wasn't going to happen.

I swallowed Will's comments willingly as I drove to meet D. The weekend had included, after all, so much pondering. Talking with Emily on the phone, recalling her experience of being lied to. (I did suspect D was lying about some little things here and there, just by the way he dodged certain follow-up questions or fudged dates about something I'd been certain he'd said.) "You're really intuitive, Val," Emily had said to me. "Follow your gut instinct on this guy." That had felt good on two levels. One, it confirmed that I had something to say about my experience and wasn't tied to some moving van driving down the road with no brakes. D's relative closedness might be just geekiness (fine with me). Or it might be wounds from divorce and widowhood (also fine or understandable). But it might also be patterns of behavior that he'd formed from his personality combined with hard times, perhaps as a protective instinct after getting hurt. That, in the end, didn't feel all that fine for building intimacy. And I certainly wasn't about to play the emotional savior or mother to anyone. Not like he'd want me to—he'd made that clear.

So the clarity came over the weekend even though I had really warmed to the potential for life partnership that looked quieter than my earlier marriage. At dinner with Kathy last week, it was so fun to recount practical things D had done that felt caring, supportive, and at least symbolic of a type of man I could spend my future with. She lovingly listened and nodded without questioning my appreciation for little gestures of his, like asking my height to make sure he brought a bike I could use (though we'd ended up walking, after all . . . but he'd been gracious).

Tuesday morning after getting my iced tea and chatting with D about summer camp plans for the kids, I asked if I could dive right into something.

"Be my guest," he said.

And then my short speech: "I've really enjoyed our times together. But I've been doing some more thinking, and I realize I'm not finding the connection I'm looking for, so I think it's time for me to move on." He responded something like same for him, which might be true.

And when he asked what I wanted to do right then, I said, "I'd like to thank you for our outings and bid each other well."

Humorous side note: We'd stopped on the sidewalk to talk, and there was a white utility van right there with the passenger-side window down and a man inside. His partner must've been grabbing a coffee at Starbucks or something. He was literally three feet away from us, so he had to have heard every word we were saying.

"It's hard for people like us," D said. But inside I was thinking, there's that pessimism I don't think I can embrace. Outwardly, I just smiled. We hugged and each turned our own way to depart.

Done!

I had this feeling walking back to my car that I'm an adult. That was an adult interaction with adult stakes and adult cordiality and adult perspective that something wasn't quite working out. It felt adult in the best sense of the word—no temper tantrums or childish demands or blaming. Just two people parting ways after exploring a connection together. Boy, was I thankful.

Last night I got back online, posted several more photos of myself and updated my profile. I took out the bit in my opening paragraph about being a widow. I'm not hiding it at all, but I want to see if I'll get some bites from people who might have been scared by an initial statement so stark. We'll see. Widowhood is a big part of my story, but unlike D, I think, it's not necessarily the whole or dominant story. Precious and eternally relevant, yes. Formative for me and the kids, yes. But dominant and defining forever, making it impossible to embrace love and joy again? We'll have to find out.

Chapter Ten

Something Remarkable Happened to My Parents

September 2014

My mom had a stroke while I was on vacation with the kids last month. My dad, who's been taking care of her 24/7, didn't recognize the symptoms immediately because her mental health has been on the decline for years, and sometimes she spaces out. So, when she was staring at her sandwich at their favorite corner bakery, he thought, *It's the Alzheimer's*. And when she couldn't track with his China pictures on the couch later, *It's the Alzheimer's*. But that evening when she trudged across their bedroom with a really weird gait, it struck him enough to call my doctor sister, who said to get mom to the ER immediately as it was probably a stroke.

So now she's home again with professional 24/7 care from people who come into my childhood home and are trained to sit with, change, wipe and hold people like my mom. Thankfully Mom can walk—at least for now—by linking arms with my dad or others. That's a biggie. But as I realize she doesn't know for sure who I am anymore, I wonder if I've said goodbye enough.

Dad is increasingly convinced it's his destiny to care for her in her sickness and old age. He's so locked into this destiny thing that he's given up everything except Monday and Wednesday bowling. ("Don't touch the bowling" would be his T-shirt.) This connection they have is not only sweet as a continuation of their fifty-year marriage but is—dare I say—miraculous.

You see, when I was a kid, I used to wonder if my parents should divorce. I sometimes wished for it. Despite growing up at a time when Susie-with-divorced-parents was still picked up by her dad from school to almost scandalized whispers, I didn't have a strong opinion about the whole idea of marriage forever. It seemed to me that if something was working, then it was working. But if people were making each other miserable, well, that didn't seem like what loving each other was about.

On the making each other miserable front, my parents yelled at each other a lot. And by a lot, I mean a lot. I'd often end up crouching in the hamper or hiding under my sheets late at night while stuff was going on that I shouldn't hear. And so what I remember thinking was, *I'm so proud of my parents for all they're doing for us and thankful for our financial stability, but I just wish they were happy. If they could help make each other happy, great. If not, well, then we'd probably be okay with another option.*

Fast-forward several decades. My parents now had four adult daughters and nine grandchildren and lots of time on their hands. Refugee and immigration stresses were a thing of the past. Jobs and earning income were done. Friends were loyal and local. And somehow, they'd learned to get along.

They'd stopped yelling. (At least most of the time—there were still periodic, heated counseling sessions that they asked me and Andrew to hold for them during our visits, but even that felt different because they were actually addressing the real issues instead of mudslinging.) And they enjoyed themselves dandily going from choir practice to Hollywood Bowl concerts to walks on the beach. My parents! Walks on the beach! Like regular retired Southern-California Americans!

So when I got the message about Mom in my hotel room the morning after the stroke, I cried for my parents and for all of us but I was also grateful. Even though the worst might be just around the corner, I was so happy she was with my dad and would be well-loved by her husband and by caregivers trained to hold her underwear as she fished with her foot to put them on.

I'm sure it sucks to have someone else help you put your underwear on. "This is the end of life," my dad says, with the tender resignation of an octogenarian who's buried half his closest friends. But he's openly grateful for a full life. He really enjoyed his career advancement. He's scarred and empowered by wartime survival. And increasingly, he acknowledges his rich life wouldn't have been possible without this woman who's now a shriveled version of her former, feisty self. My mom cries when I mention that dad loves her, which makes me think that improving your marriage in your late seventies can't be all bad. The other day she turned to one of the ladies who was feeding her and said, "This is all so great. You have to stay with my husband and me, and I'm going to make you another one of my daughters."

If I have to lose my mind someday, I'd love to do it my mom's way—caught up in how good life is and eager to share my marriage and home with even more people. And I'd love to copy my dad, too—bowling, for sure, but also still sitting on that couch next to her with nowhere else he'd rather be.

Chapter Eleven

Meeting James

November 2015

W e met over a dating app called "Coffee Meets Bagel." It's a simple phone app that feeds users just one match per day at noon. No scrolling through the masses as if comparing cleaning products. I must say, for all the downsides of Facebook algorithms and election manipulation shit from 2016, I am grateful for some brilliant uses of data sharing. By suggesting whom I might enjoy meeting through my Facebook "Friends of Friends," Coffee Meets Bagel felt like a digital buddy setting up a blind date.

As an online dating moron, I didn't banter on text as I should have. Instead, I picked up his "accepted" status indicating he, too, had swiped right, so to speak, and sent a message to meet the next day. "Hi James, I'm Val. Nice to meet you. I'm heading to sleep now, but would you like to meet up tomorrow?" Apparently in the dating world, that is the equivalent of putting your dry ingredients directly into the oven—no liquids, no mixing, just set the timer for thirty minutes.

James went along with it, though, no push back. His suggestion to meet up Friday around 2:00 p.m. didn't work for me, given school pick-up times. So while I was in the community health center the next morning dealing with another insurance blow-up, I messaged him asking if 10:00 a.m. would work instead.

"Sure," he typed back, "no big deal. The afternoon was just a random time I threw out to pick something."

For some reason, I liked that sentence a lot. It was so unpackaged, just a down-to-earth thing someone would say about finding a time to meet. Plus, since James's online photos hadn't sported a huge bare chest, I figured we were already at two points.

I coached myself after parking across the street from the Cambridge Library Starbucks.

Feed the meter, take a breath, remember you'll live through anything. Just don't get in a car with him today.

I could see a tiny stream of coffee-seekers wandering in and out of Starbucks's door. There was just enough of a people-flow to feel socially okay if I had to stand there waiting until he arrived.

But I didn't wait. As I strode up, he walked up exactly at that moment from the other direction. Blue micro down jacket. Glasses. Smiling. Nice-looking. I shot out my arm like a robot who's programmed to forbid hugs.

"Nice to meet you." I smiled back.

He gave a chuckle and shook my hand, then gestured for me to walk in front of him toward the door. It's something I have now seen him do countless times just before he opens the door for me. What is it about small acts of kindness? He also does this for a parent with a stroller, a person with packages to carry on the bus, a toddler dropping a binkie. He lets others go first.

The small stream of customers had formed a line about seven long. My initial thought was that it might be awkward standing there. But concern dissolved as James asked how parking went for me. "Better than I thought," I replied, to which he quipped back that the vicious meter maids of Cambridge weren't out that day, then. A real laugh came out of my mouth without pause. This, too, I now recognize as a daily occurrence with James, that exhaling of stress in a moment of levity. But in that moment, I was delighted. A man on a first date was funny without trying too hard!

Well, given that I'm telling this story in fond retrospect, it's easy to see all the signs pointing in one direction. Of course, I've had my endless angst about everything James-related. And I'll do that out loud here again in a moment. But that Friday, it did strike me as we sat drinking Youthberry tea on a bench outside the library, how completely at ease I felt. Of course, I was aware that I was on a date and had put on a black jacket I thought looked good with my hair even though it made me fidget. But I was actually having fun for the entire hour. I swear, the skies were even unseasonably blue, and only friendly bikers rode past us, obeying traffic signs. A big bonus was that I was blissfully unaware that I had freaked James out by mentioning I'd been a church pastor until that summer. It turns out he'd immediately started to write me off since he'd also been a pastor and assumed I'd be like too many judgmental others he'd known. Audibly, he only replied, "Oh, really." (As he later reported to me, it helped a lot that I swore during the first date as well, dropping an f-bomb while talking on our bench. I guess it functioned for James as a kind of pH balance to my hyper-religious job. Thank God for f-bombs.)

Our second date was two days later, a four-hour sandwich dinner at Parish Cafe in Boston's Back Bay. Midway through the meal, after James announced his passion for meatloaf, we played a get-to-know-you game. It involved taking turns asking questions about each other's lives. James smirked after a few rounds, and then asked a real killer of a question: "What question do you not want me to ask you?" I considered, then told him the truth. I didn't want him to ask me if I was having a good time. Because I was having a terrific time, and terrified about it.

The date ended with what I consider a fairy-tale first kiss on Copley Plaza. Then a second one as we parted on the train platform. That one floated me home, awakened from some kind of widow coma. Me, an only parent accustomed to muddy cleats and greasy Tupperware, having recently graduated from wiping butts. From wind-up to pitch, complete with middle-of-the-plate connection on a solid swing, I got a picture-perfect first kiss. (By the way, you just got my best baseball vocabulary from eleven years of watching Little League and listening to Jerry Remy recap Sox plays on WEEI Boston.) The whole event far surpassed my expectations and even now deserves some kind of Sundance award in my mind for uncheesy cheesiest beginnings.

I went home and basically became a teenager again, obsessed with my crush. I was still a mom, of course. I had two middle schoolers going to bed later than I'd been used to. So,

I waited until their bedtimes, and then I curled up in an armchair in the corner of the dining room to talk on the phone most nights. Remember the days of phone cords pulled as far as they could stretch so that you could close the door and not let your parents hear your conversation? Same, but sub out the parents for your kids (laughing–crying emoji).

Thanksgiving came, and James and I were texting daily now and seeing each other a couple of times each week. We aimed for evenings when I could either a) get coverage from the grandparents, who were generous with their time, or b) leave the oldest in charge, hoping he'd turn off the stove. I cooked for the boys most of those nights I went out. It was a bit manic, really. I think I had to prove to myself I was not abandoning my children just because my libido was now in high gear. God forbid they'd someday tell a therapist, "Our dad died, and our mom was super available for a while, but then one year, she suddenly had to run out the door for kisses . . ." Whether that was true or not, the kids were at an easy age that year where the oldest was simply happy to be put in charge, the middle was in that flexible (if slightly to his own disadvantage) balanced mindset, and the youngest was just so tickled that they could watch TV in the middle of the week. It was, looking back, a sort of perfect window for me to start dating.

As fast as the rush of romance came, so too did the scary unknowns. I wrote the following journal entries during the first month:

11/17/2015

I'm searching for meaning to go with my heart beating and open. Is it plain and simple, Lord? Is it green light go? And what's his value on honesty? Does he ever lie? What's up with his profile pics that look so different from each other?

11/23/2015

My heart is breaking
  as I remember how it used to be:
I walked among the crowds of worshipers,
  leading a great procession to the house of God,
singing for joy and giving thanks
  amid the sound of a great celebration!
Why am I discouraged?
  Why is my heart so sad?
I will put my hope in God!
  I will praise him again . . .
—Psalm 42:4-5, New Living Translation

Is there a bit of longing for the past, or does the psalmist recall those previous happy times to increase faith for future happy times? Not sure. But today, I take that as a bit of a warning of where I don't want to get stuck—in the past.

I've been grieving "my former happy life." It's especially hard when realizing I met Andrew when we were twenty. The brokenness from youth felt less crystallized. Glaring, yes, but somehow more forgivable. What does it mean when you meet people in midlife and those flaws haven't all been healed?

11/24/2015

Seeing James tonight. Have a bad feeling about things.

11/28/2015

James. Who are you?

Within a very short time, I experienced bouts of paralyzing fear when James said things that coincidentally matched up with themes I'd been talking about that week with my girlfriends or sisters. Surely he must be tapping my phone or house. Otherwise, why would he mention Anne Hathaway the very same evening I'd been watching an Anne Hathaway movie? And why did he use the phrase "six of one, half a dozen of another" the day after I'd used it—an idiom I rarely utter? During those phone calls, my end of the line went dead, leaving James in confused waiting. Sometimes I managed to revive the conversation, forcing myself to talk about anything lighter than my fear that he was a sociopath stalker. Other times, I simply ended the call and told him I was sorry I couldn't talk longer.

My therapist, Mary, who I began seeing as a result of these terrors, said likely it was PTSD. She took stock of what I'd written down as suspicious occurrences. Except for one detail, which she acknowledged was strange timing, Mary told me that nothing seemed outside the realm of sheer chance. Coincidences do happen.

"But should I cut things off with him since you raised your eyebrows at that one detail?" I pressed her.

"No," she answered. "Instead, could you be overlaying the fact you were deceived by friends in the past who wore a mask of charm to cover their lies?"

Mary repeatedly reminded me, "James is not 'Madoff.'" And at times, her coaching worked. I lasted through phone calls. I also met James's friends. They seemed sane and altogether generous, hosting us at their house one evening when one was about to give birth any minute. They looked me in the eye, knowing I was collecting data as a single mom who was dating, which automatically jacked up my radar. "He's a good guy," Mike reassured me, all joking of the evening aside as we snuck in a serious moment as James used their restroom.

My friends did the same. Liz and Hiromu hosted our faithful dinner group to meet James, since Jess had told us of a meet-the-boyfriend that happened a bit late for another friend. As Liz went to the kitchen to get her sumptuous dessert, the others friendly-grilled James by way of probing just a little, smiling a lot, and asking him what he liked about me. His answers produced a charge to me soon thereafter from Scott: "Be good to James. He's my man." (Any time your own friend with a heart of gold tells you to treat with kindness a guy he just met, that makes you highly esteem your new boyfriend and settle in for the ride.) These encouragements came often enough to help me relax in between the freak-outs.

Meanwhile, being a mom didn't escape my fluttering heart. I suggested to James he meet my boys while the stakes were low. I asked him one day after we took a long walk at the Chestnut Hill Reservoir and sat in my car while it poured outside.

He didn't hesitate. "No." He drew out the "o" as if he was repeating the word.

My eyes grew wide, and James explained. It was actually a "not yet." His reasoning was that my kids had lost their father. Should our relationship, just over a month old, fail to take hold but the boys already bonded to him, his departure would be another loss of a man in their life.

"We need to see if we really get along first," he added warmly, setting our course for the next few months. The waiting killed me on the one hand, as someone who lacks patience for things I perceive as good ends. But a James answer that's firm comes less often, and I quickly recognized it for what it was—wise. The silver lining of waiting was a rich connection. Who doesn't want to dine out with a gentlemanly, smart, goofy, and inquisitive date who likes you? Who wouldn't want hand-holding walks across the Mass. Ave. Bridge, with blustery winds prompting excuses to stop and embrace while gazing at Boston's beautiful skyline? We did everything from playing Yahtzee (I let him Yahtz-splain the dice game to me) to sharing pie at Trident Cafe. I soaked in the harmonious adult company, also aware of our differences and my resulting questions.

All the while, I wrote and talked to God in my journal. The questions I was wrestling with were equal parts James-centric and the general terror of emotional intimacy. With Andrew, I'd met and married a guy whose personhood I got to know largely embedded within a public sphere. From the beginning to the end of our marriage, we developed a friendship that seemed to always have three, or even thirty or three hundred, other people in the room. From the time we arrived in Massachusetts as newlyweds in 1997, we volunteered and then worked for a church start-up that went from 35 people to nearly 1,000 congregants within a decade. Almost every hour of our spare time was devoted to meetings, shopping for stuff, cooking, reading, writing, praying, speaking, counseling folks, and attending conferences. Multiple nights and weekends for work were a given, a mostly joyful assumption of putting the mission first. It was all part of the deal, a fishbowl into which we birthed and started raising our three sons. I am incredibly thankful for the experience, but it also prevented me from immersing myself in the quiet delight and risk of being in love.

12/28/2015

Go before me, Lord God.

The Lord is my Shepherd, I lack in nothing.
You make me lie down in green pastures,
You lead me beside still waters, You restore my soul.
You lead me in paths of righteousness for your name's sake.
Even though I walk through the shadows of the valley of death, I fear
no evil, for You are with me. Your rod and your staff, they comfort me.
You prepare a table in front of me in the presence of my enemies.
You anoint my head with oil;
My cup overflows.
Surely goodness and mercy will follow me all the days of my life,
And I will dwell in the house of the Lord
forever.
—Psalm 23, paraphrased from the Bible, New International Version

FAREWELL TO DISNEYLAND · 115

Amen. Let me rejoice in Your abundant goodness, which also gives me confidence to love again.

12/31/2015

I'm afraid I'm still in grief—somehow trapped in introspection or seriousness. When faced with a real, live person like James who's ready for relationship, I toggle back and forth between wanting to grow in connection and run away.

Scared I'll be in a funk tonight and need liquor to loosen up (but then maybe too much). Scared of letting my guard down with James. Scared of him not being trustworthy. Scared of bad surprises. Excited because of the connection. Grateful he's interested. Uncertain of who he is.

That night walking to The Buttery, I wondered to you about James. It seemed that you answered me, "This is my beloved son, in whom I'm well pleased."

2/21/2016

James and I are still together. Was struck in church how I can scapegoat what happened with the "Madoffs" when afraid of getting close to James. It's true: I have traumatic stress from that whole debacle. But it's time to inch closer to James and allow him in more.

From Ivy's sermon at church this morning: "Assume people are profoundly beautiful and profoundly broken, both."

Mary the therapist seemed unflappable in her insistence that James was flawed but that it didn't make him a bad man. For some reason, her point bothered me. Since she was unconcerned that he might be a sociopath, shouldn't she soon have an explanation or remedy for some of his bothersome behaviors? Shouldn't part of the result of counseling for relationships be a sunny path forward, sprinkled with healing herbs for midlife character ills with a fresh mound of community service on the side? Whenever I got upset about things James had done or not done, she looked at me and said, "He's human. And he's flawed. And so are you."

Wasn't that the rub? I was having a hard time accepting that I was dating a real human being. But slowly, slowly, I listened to Mary. And I kept collecting data in my mind. And I played more Yahtzee.

3/4/2016

Basically totally smitten with James. That's ITMO— in the midst of—very real adult serious weighty things.

Jesus, thank you so very much for James. Thank you for giving me permission to pursue joy and fulfillment. Yes, sacrifice is a season—and it was a very long season for me:

1997: Church planting
2002: Having babies
2008: Andrew's illness
2010: Widowhood

And then, rather suddenly in October 2015,* I find myself graciously free. In a green pasture. With James, who tends to my thoughts and feelings so kindly and generously. How lucky am I? Will this all come to a screeching halt someday?

But no, I say. Even if I lose James, I will celebrate now and try, as he says, to float down the stream. I laugh as I think about him saying about our situation:

"I'm floating down the stream, and we'll see where it takes us."

And I, answering,
"But why can't we paddle down the stream?"
So we shall see, indeed.

We shall see.

*I finished my pastor job in August 2015, and by the end of October, my to-do lists became more doable. I had five piano students that first month, and, as an old friend once said with understated profundity, I had time to stare out the window.

Chapter Twelve

Mother's Day 2017

Yesterday afternoon, I toasted four other glasses at a terrific restaurant in Boston. I had a lovely day feeling celebrated, and the joy of speaking to my mom, as well.

Of course, as with all holidays, I got provoked to think about the day's significance. Days marked on calendars bring more richness, more pain, more surprises, and more unfinished business and things out of my control with each passing year. Yesterday was no different.

For the first time in seven years, my three sons had the man I love prompting them to make cards and breakfast for me. (Yesterday's breakfast, by the way, is still making me the happiest mom around, all the way to the artery-replacement aisle.) Cards appeared in the morning that were 3-D, or poetic, or edited versions of other creations. In previous years, either because of their age or lackadaisical inattention to completion, the cards were hilarious or somewhat of a letdown. I treasured the other cards, too, but this year felt different. I surveyed the four pairs of eyes staring expectantly at me, and there were not only the pleased looks of children proud and tired from their morning's work but the question mark in James's eyes. *Is this okay? I hope you like it.*

I surely did like it. How could I not? First was the gentle surprise of having another adult at the Mother's Day table, which caught me off-guard. I felt so relaxed. When you love and then lose love, you hold your chin up to be brave for others and swear off self-pity even while gathering friends to hear you freak out regularly. At least that's what I did. Others fall into different patterns of grief, letting things out or allowing others into their hearts sooner or going at it more alone, just generally stumbling along a different meandering, obscured path, week by week into years. Something bonds us, though: nothing will ever be the same, and whether we are okay or not replaces the question of whether everything is as it should be.

No, even with the joy of five glasses toasting together again, everything is not as it should be. Others we love are not with us, and hopes hovering at 10% fulfilled remain. There are the patterns we've created as a result of living with loss, that we wonder if we can ever rejigger. But I am more than okay. Increasingly, I can put one foot in front of the other on a path that is well-lit enough for the next step. Not only that, but the company along it both near and far is the best and most loving company I know. This must be God's investment in us; this must be part of life in its fullness. And this must speak to a forever after that is far more intricate than I'd imagined when I was drawing pots of gold at age eight. The rain still falls sometimes while the rainbow shines. But, I reluctantly admit, light and colors are more glorious set against those storm clouds.

Chapter Thirteen

How God Plays into Things for Me

1972–2018

I've had a very longtime relationship to God, whom I address with a capital G as a name to an actual divine person, that I should probably explain just so you know where I'm coming from in all my musings. Things have been evolving ever since Andrew died but in ways that seem to provoke all my unanswered questions from years way, way before that. It's funny how grief, and even good news like getting married again, stir the pot of all the bad news and the questions. One new little emergence is a perspective that I can live out my God connection without the need to tie it all together with a neat bow.

My God relationship started when Henry and Marilyn Ting, to my memory a young and not particularly well-to-do couple, decided to hang out with kids from my church when I was eight. I'd attended a church before that, but from those early years I mostly remember the amazing lunches my family would eat in Chinatown every Sunday after church, followed by MSG-induced episodes of hysterical laughter at the restaurant table, followed by sisters lolling in a food coma in the back seat on the long drive home. That ride was much better than the vomiting episodes on the way to church, which involved passing a bag while driving on Interstate 5. How I didn't hate church just for the association with vomit every week is a wonder. But that's another story.

So back to God and the Tings. Henry and Marilyn, whom I called "Uncle" and "Auntie" out of loving respect that's common in Chinese culture, invited our church class to their apartment building, where they'd let us swim in the pool. After that, we would sit in their living room and eat yummy snacks. In my kid memory, the spread was some glorious mix of gummy worms, pizza rolls, and towers of brownies topped with marshmallows. Maybe it was just Fritos, but good enough. It struck me the whole while that they never minded (or at least never said they minded) the fact that we sat on their furniture with wet chlorine-soaked butts. Mind you, this was in 1980 when chlorine was king, and no one gave any thought to natural pool cleaners. So our butts were fully greeny chloriney, and I'm sure none of us really dried off before plunking down on their sofa.

Henry and Marilyn were both quiet people; still are to this day in grandparenthood. They never pushed any doctrine on us. And they put up with a boy named Tom who literally climbed under the table every time they took us out to IHOP for breakfast as a church class. (I kid you not—he did this so much we called him "Tom under the Table." Worse, it was under an IHOP table. Gross.) Therefore, it simply seemed obvious to me that the God whom they claimed loved us was just like Henry and Marilyn. So later when they introduced Jesus to me, saying Jesus loves you, I thought, *Well, sure, if Jesus would let me go swimming and sit with my wet butt on his couch and talk about whatever I wanted at his apartment and eat pizza rolls, I'll get to know him.* Ten-year-old Val started a journey that led to many mini-journeys and sub-plots and lessons learned about what religion can and can't do. But in all of it, I never lost the sense that there is a Someone who I call God, or Jesus, and that I'd rather go through life with this Person than not. For sure. Hence why my relating to God keeps popping up when hard things happen like cancer or betrayal or parenthood or embarrassing things like flirtations gone ridiculously wrong.

My story is my story, of course. I fully recognize that when we're subject to really negative and damaging parenting or just other crap, that makes it pretty hard not to see any god as a despot or absent druggie or pissed off power tripper. I'm a person who went to church as a kid where a young couple treated her nicely. And something about their kindness offset the yelling going on at home and helped me connect with a loving Mother-Father God figure. It's different from my sister, whose supposed best friend in eighth grade was bitchy to her at the church youth group, which pretty much turned her off from the whole Christian deal. Or from my Jewish neighbors who sold me their leaven one Passover and taught me about godly rest and laughter on the Shabbat. (I'll be a token Gentile for them anytime.) Or from the Muslim neighbors with whom my church shares an Iftar dinner and soccer camp for 200 kids every summer. But whatever the specifics, it's cool to think that reaching out or reaching up in crisis brings us peace and connection with Someone-who-loves-us, as opposed to leaving us shaking our fists.

Of course, you might ask what happened to all that reaching out and reaching up when the shit hit the fan for my family.

I've talked with a lot of people who went through cancer or other hard stuff, and some had nothing good to say about divine anything. Fair enough. I sympathize with their understandable anger at the unfair way life works. And yet for years, I never quite understood the sentiment that everything changed about God in their view just because bad stuff happened. God was good as long as life was good, but hey, something shitty happened and so now God was shit, too. As I saw it, every sacred text of every permutation of faith in the world had been written during some epoch of actual world history. And world history, to my best recollection, had massive problems and boatloads of injustice and pain. So if one sacred text was promoting a God helpful for life's problems, it was talking about help in the midst of the pain of life, not in its absence. From a Christian vantage point, Jesus, after all, lived when people were getting dragged into arenas to be ripped apart by lions. How did that 1st century widow in Rome feel about her hubby being fed to the lions, I wonder? A weird and extreme example, perhaps, but helpful to me when considering whether faith can endure through various evils such as cancer.

I did change at some point, however, my notions of how God works in the world. I was helped by the thesis of a book called *Is God to Blame?* by Gregory Boyd. It's a somewhat repetitive book, I discovered in a book club with friends. And it's written with assumptions of a certain kind of religious readership. But Boyd had a pretty powerful bottom line about pain. He said we all walk around thinking God is unknowable and the world is easy to figure out. He argues it's the opposite. Reality is, we can't control almost anything in the world— weather, or cars, or other people, and certainly not terrible diseases. Boyd posits there's spiritually charged shit flying around all the time that we cannot see that affects us. So that's a mystery about the world we need to accept if we want to have faith of any kind. In other words, we are very small. He laments in chapter after chapter about how some religious practice does no favors to authentic faith by claiming you can confidently know everything. Most people in the world NOT from North America or other "first-world" groups accept the uncontrollable nature of the universe, he argues. Good point, Greg.

Boyd goes on to say that God, at least as revealed in sacred books, is actually pretty interested in being personally known and not that shrouded in mystery. The Jesus who hung out with prostitutes when the religious establishment condemned him for that choice was demonstrating he was an amazingly accepting guy. The God who created ancient cross-cultural families from messed-up people and promoted justice across class was a powerful reconciler in society. That God, Boyd argues, wouldn't do something like stick cancer in your spouse because he somehow wanted the good ones to "come home to heaven sooner." On the other hand, he argues that the mysterious forces in a spiritually charged universe would totally mess with your health or your happiness. Or spark genocide and other large-scale atrocities. So, one of course wonders, is God really a nice grandparent? S/he's kind but powerless? No, Boyd says (in much more eloquent terms than mine); s/he has utmost power. But God chose to make a universe where people are not robots but free to do good or bad. It's freedom that makes true love and powerfully influential choices that battle evil possible, which is essential to being human. Take a God who is entirely in charge of every bit of world events, and you have human robots serving a puppet master. Exchange a robotic, trouble-free reality for love and freedom to choose, and you have a messy world.

After reading Boyd, I decided I'll buy that theory about shit happening, at least as much as I buy any other why-does-evil-exist-in-the-universe theory.

During crisis and early widowhood, I was reminded of this simple line in the Bible which gave me practical ways to engage my faith. It said, "To everyone who asks, it will be given." And, "If you ask God for bread, God won't give you a stone." I tried it despite my pride. When we needed help for rides, I mentioned that to people when they said they wanted to help. I even mentioned it when they might have said it just to get off the phone (which would've been fine).

"I should probably go . . . Is there anything you need help with this week?" they'd ask.

"Well, since you offered," I'd venture, "Wednesday Andrew has an appointment at the hospital and I have to take the boys to baseball practice. Would you be willing to drive him?"

And almost every time, with only a few instances of feeling that really awkward pause, I'd get what I needed. So I kept asking God and people for help, like a Pavlovian dog who liked the snacks that came when the bell rang.

The feedback I got when trying faith out with practical needs was good enough that I tried it when I was feeling emotionally needy, as well. In moments of intense emotion around loss and change, I tried crying and saying out loud exactly what I was thinking, imagining God to be in front of me while I did it. What came out were weird and honest things, not necessarily noble things. For example, I remember being frustrated at the hospital with Andrew one day while he was getting injected with drugs. We were sitting in the chemo infusion room having a conversation about some urgent job stuff. And we couldn't finish because his heart started racing and his blood pressure shot up the longer our conversation went on. His awesome chemo nurse Teresa (who was twenty-something but as wise, calm, and loving as the turtle Oogway in *Kung Fu Panda*) gave me a hard stare when she saw his spiking vital signs, and we immediately changed the subject. You'd think any good wife would be completely absorbed by the alarming nature of the moment, medically speaking. My attention should've been entirely focused on the well-being of my suffering spouse. But what I found myself praying to God was actually a vent, something like:

God, I'm so frustrated that Andrew and I can't talk about work like we used to. I'm so pissed and disappointed I've lost my processing partner.

And in that immediate moment, I sensed a God-voice-in-my-head confirm that notion with this response: *Yes, you are. And yes, you have.*

And those prayer moments were super validating and satisfying. In part what those interactions did for me was drive home that I was actually going through something real. Cancer was impacting my life, and God seemed to have sympathy like a friend does. It didn't seem as surreal then that I was "talking to God" or he was "talking to me," even though writing about it does seem kind of crazy. All I know is, I didn't come up with those things to say on my own, and God seemed nicer than I would've been to myself, quite honestly. On top of that, I felt immensely grounded after our little chats. Despite believing that God did have the power to spontaneously heal people, as I'd heard instances from people I personally knew, I got the feeling that our family's story was not to be so simple as that. (Sigh.) So when I vented to God about my feelings, the best part was that I received a witness to my experience. This Witness, I believed in my moments of most intense emotion, did not offer me advice but rather a steady Wise Presence. Sometimes, I felt like God just confirmed that what I was living was real, as a great friend would. Just like the practical ways we received help when I asked for it, I found that God's presence and friendship very personally comforting. So I pursued even more of this mystical practice.

Practicing God's presence wasn't entirely new to me going through cancer with Andrew and then his death. I'd had a vision back when I was a decade-younger woman teaching history to high schoolers but hating my chosen career path. My sentiment had nothing to do with the very kind supervisor or reasonably great kids I got to teach or the very interesting subject matter. It had mostly to do with the fact I was a newlywed, freshly moved across the country with unrealistic pressure in my young, well-educated head to change the world. But rather than gaining perspective, I hated every day more and more, and spent numerous hours crashing in front of the TV after work. Andrew, himself stuck in graduate school and a low-paying job, got increasingly worried.

I was awake one night in the apartment we had rented sight-unseen. We were lying below the bedroom windows that still had Andrew's high school bedsheets with purple, orange, turquoise, and black stripes flung up as makeshift curtains. It was about 3:30 a.m., and I was in such a state that I was on my hands and knees on the mattress like a standing dog as Andrew slept next to me. I was rocking back and forth, seized with anxiety about facing the high schoolers in just four hours. Into my head popped the idea that I could reach up from my pit of despair. And in the exact moment I decided to try it, a vision of Jesus came into my head. But it was so big, it was really as if he filled the whole bed in front of me, kind of superimposed on top of my sleeping husband. I saw Jesus sitting in a lawn chair, a kind of Adirondack chair all low to the ground. He was leaning back in a relaxed manner as if holding a cold beer in one hand and just hanging out at someone's backyard BBQ. When I saw him, he asked me (although I don't recall his lips moving, I knew he was asking me),

"What do you want me to do for you?"

(For anybody familiar with that story where Jesus asks a disabled beggar the same question just before healing him, it had that feel.) I answered from the bottom of my heart,

"I want to be happy."

I felt him ask back, "What will make you happy?"

And it suddenly crystallized for me like a prison key suddenly floating in the air just outside my cell door:

Quitting.

Now mind you, this is not rocket science, especially in today's job patterns. Hate your job? Leave it! Two years somewhere? That's forever! But to me, a daughter of immigrant parents, who had drilled into her that getting what you want involves endless perseverance, quitting was far from an easy sell. So that night, for me to picture Jesus inviting me to entertain quitting was truly startling. An idea that I would never have come up with on my own, not only because I had parental influence on the brain but because I had 35K of debt from my master's program in education. That suggestion, to my mind, could only be from an outside influence. And since I was staring at a vision of Jesus, I considered this influence to come from him.

Oh well, I thought, *if all else fails I can blame none other than Jesus Christ for allowing me to quit.* So I gave notice and did my best to finish out my time with the kids and staff and paperwork. And then I worked temp jobs and ultimately landed in work that was a much better fit for a very long time. In the meantime, a couple of friends who scored it big on the stock market offered to pay off my grad school debt (#wut). Not provide a loan, mind you, but just a gift of paying it off. Something about their observing the ancient practice of the "Year of Jubilee," where the historic Israelites allowed debtors to clear the slate every fifty years, which I guess was that particular year. With both of these confirming events—the debt being paid off and the new work being a great fit—I did have the feeling that that vision I'd had back on my mattress was the real deal.

I found I still resonated with that idea of God being on my side when Andrew died. For his funeral slideshow, I picked a photo of him toasting me in Italy. Andrew's smile in that moment seemed rather timeless. It appeared less the static picture of a dead man and more a forever kind of smile that was free from pain and had moved on to the next life. What Andrew would look like in a super-duper new cancer-free body, I had no idea. But I did sense that God was behind it, this glorious new phase of life my husband would encounter, one that wasn't trapped by endless needles and appointments and the banal lists of earthly crap of managing disease or daily chores. Or who knows: maybe he and David Foster Wallace were zooming around the world together, sprinkling fairy dust on grocery store checkout lines. I sensed that this happy funeral photo was some kind of freeze frame of Andrew's new norm. He was somewhere having a great cuppa joe, and then another, and then moving on to compare microbrews and debate the finer points of seared tuna. Andrew had won in some cosmic sense, with a God at his back who wanted him to win the whole time. It was awful for the boys' sake and mine that cancer had beat us in the battle, but Andrew was undefeated in the global sense that spanned over all future Time. I embrace that experience of the ever after and of a good Person who'll see us to the realer end.

Funnily enough, faith's been a stranger friend as life calmed down and my family entered the years known as "just living." God's absence is now also as real as her presence. I see that in death, in longing, in disappointment, in acceptance, there is no longer an ability to force-fit God into my notion of a highly idealized life. God being good doesn't mean that everything works out the way I thought it should. And yet, concluding he is bad or doesn't exist doesn't seem right to me, either. I've had my share of recent prayers that seem to have been answered in profoundly meaningful, concrete ways, including a major career shift that came too easily, kids growing up okay so far, and even meeting my fiancé under striking circumstances for us both. That motivates me to continue beating on the drum of things like prayer and asking for peace and purpose, as well as counting my blessings and telling God thanks every chance I get. But then, real heartache over our losses continues to haunt my whole family such that I sometimes get glazed over and just want to zone out, watching movies on Netflix like *"This is 40"* while being jealous of how Leslie Mann looks in a skirt. I'm hopeful that by the time I'm 80, I'll be all aglow with visionary passion about the world and God and purpose again. That would fit my notion of ending life with a kickass attitude.

For now, I try to love. I try to plug away at my tasks. And I still reach out in many moments to say, basically,

"You still there?"

And I feel like what I get back is,

"Yep."

Chapter Fourteen

Let's Cross to the Other Side, Said Jesus

December 2017

I'm engaged, but I'm terrified of getting married again.

This moment comes, that horizon with the happily-ever-after theoretically dancing upon it, but it doesn't look like a happily-ever-after. It looks like committing to a lot of scary possibilities of what could go wrong again, enduring constant compromise, managing irritation with well-set behaviors, and feeling stretched between that well-controlled single life and giving up control. Going through my brain, along with gratitude, is the concession, *"Maybe this is good enough?"*

And besides terrifying, it's a smack in the face. At forty-five, you'd think I'd have gotten a long visit from Wisdom and her sister Realistic Expectations and that my Disney-raised philosophy about relationships might've faded by now. After all, not only was I widowed in my thirties—a harsh reality no matter how much support you get—but I was married, after all, to an imperfect man whose flaws did affect me and our kids.

Nope.

This time around, marriage still seems like it should promise a perfectly happy ending, and I'm fighting the fact that it won't be.

Now, don't get me wrong. There are many, many, many awesome things that I listed off just yesterday (after listing them off the week before, and the month before that, ad infinitum) in my journal as substantial awesomeness about James, or blessings I'm experiencing with him. He has the brainy, inquisitive nature of a David Axelrod with the goofy snark of Tina Fey. He listens for what's behind my words to catch my heart, my hopes, my worries. And his advice is so often just freakin' spot-on. As for deep thoughts, his quest for understanding that shapes a personal connection to God and the world around him challenges my own mind in a way that hasn't happened in so long that I recognize it like this: *Dammit, this guy makes me grow.* And without saying too much, the man turns me on big-time. Already, in some sense, he has become my soulmate and best friend.

And my boys are consistently happy about this situation. My inquiries about their satisfaction must come off to them like the old Verizon-turned-Sprint commercial guy, as I repeatedly ask, "Are you happy now? How about now? How is it now?" Their only complaint is when James has to go home because he doesn't, despite a well-worn couch downstairs, live with us. They love hanging with him, respect his input, appreciate his help, enjoy his humor, and rib his rejection of sushi. Of course, real complaints will come, but as a starter it's been good.

But the warts that are so apparent as we speed toward fifty are less masked than when we were twenty-five. True, the years I spent with Andrew revealed warty things just as serious. In fact, had cancer not shown up and I were still married to Andrew, chances are that huge warts would've appeared in his company, or because of him. But James's and my warts are our opening lines. It's like, "Hey, I'm Val, and by the way I was betrayed by my closest friend, so in three dates I'm going to think you're lying to my face, possibly for the rest of our lives if we marry. Also, my husband died, so that health concern you mentioned makes me reel in fear that you're going to abandon me and that's tragic and so I don't think I can enjoy this taco dinner we're having." It's a tough thing to get around, this staring-down of midlife marital beginnings. My lack of trust in the man I might sleep with for good and general unease in what the future holds means a whole lot of panic, terror and generally preemptive pain.

For James, well, he has a different constellation of warts as he is a survivor of a traumatic first marriage. The young man who seems to have had endless curiosity and a gentle disposition was repeatedly beaten down. So where does that leave him? Watchful. Guarded, that's for sure. Spending a lot, and I mean a lot, of time on his phone. It's not that he doesn't consistently make efforts to love me, pursue me, and fight for us. He does, with a patience that is especially awesome in the rearview mirror. But we've both had to survive stuff.

This evening, he and I will talk about whatever is on my newest list of things I wanted to talk about. Suddenly, I'm at a loss to list the subjects off. Money is part of it. Another part is his mood last Sunday night and the mixed reaction I had to the stuff he shared. It's my questions about how he'll engage as a stepfather. It's, in many ways, my fears that I'll be left alone, even if married. That I'll be betrayed, hoodwinked, abandoned, and disappointed. Again.

As I read the Bible, a certain part I've run into a million times pops out at me this go-round. It's Jesus inviting his friends to get in a boat with him and cross to the other side of the lake. They do, and in the middle of their crossing, a big storm comes up and they freak out. Finding Jesus asleep (I love how the Bible describes him as resting on a pillow, as if to reassure readers that he wouldn't wake up with a neck kink), the friends scream, "Don't you care that we're going to drown?!"

There's the rub, it seems. They were just minding their damn business, accepted what seemed like a decent invitation, but then got caught completely out of control, fighting for their lives and feeling screwed over by the person who landed them there.

Jesus, as the storyteller summarized, told the wind and the waves to be quiet as if they were feisty toddlers yelling over the other kids in daycare. The water returned to normal, and all the friends landed on the other side and did the cool stuff he proposed they do before they got in the boat.

"Let's cross to the other side." I can imagine his hand waving a half-moon of welcome, beckoning me to join him on some new adventure. Concretely speaking, it's an invitation to forge a committed partnership within a second marriage, to invest creative energy toward new adventures and possibly a new city, all with new dreams. For me in particular, it's an invitation to life beyond being in charge all the time, being a symbolic hero to people who don't know my overwhelming fears. The other side Jesus is talking about might be the best path to living free of protecting myself from being hurt again. But like that stormy lake, crossing to the other side feels utterly like dying. I have lost control, just like when the kids wet their pants in the bookstore. There are too many factors to control. Stepchildren across the world. A hostile ex-wife. Teen children with unique challenges right under our nose. A fiancé who, like me, has buttons that get pushed.

Can I bank on Jesus's words? And can I bank on the story that ends with people living their next adventure as they intended, and not drowning instead?

Who knows; maybe a healthy second marriage is more like a first marriage should be. It's apparently limited. It's still deeply fulfilling but in a bit more distanced, I-respect-you-as-your-own-person sort of way. I'm not looking for James to be my prince entirely. (Although, in moments like me cowering in the corner after seeing a mouse last night, you can bet your ass I look forward to his princely emptying of successful traps.) But more, I mean that I'm seeing that James is as flawed a human being as I am. Health issues occasionally beset him, and disappointments shadow some of his days. He's affected by his humanity, meaning he wears the scars of life and limitations, as do I.

At the same time, James has fresh wind that can only be explained by seeing his hang-in-there spirit, and the possible favor of a God who's present with us as we trudge or skip through our days. Who can predict the future? Certainly not James nor I, as death and divorce ruined our ideals of a perfect forever-anything. Even now, as we consider anteing up again for the "I do," I imagine we both ruminate daily that there is just no guarantee. He could betray me someday. And

I could betray him. We've already hurt each other in patterns all our own doing. And death will come to us all.

So with these things in mind, I prepare to give my vows again.

Chapter Fifteen

Easter 2018

Now that my family's holiday celebrations are over, I contemplate what makes the ideal size for holiday celebrating. I'm thrown by the fact that I had only my nuclear family sitting around the table this year. And I realize I have a lopsided lifelong perspective heavily skewed in favor of massive gatherings.

When I was eight, for example, the year I wore my awesome black-and-white-with-strawberries dress for Christmas Eve, my parents invited the usual fifty people over. Then, unbeknownst to them, Auntie Betty invited her brother's family as well, which comprised Uncle Walter, his wife, and their five sons, Dave, Dale, Dick, Dean, and Dirk. Auntie Betty wasn't even a real aunt, but Chinese people do that—invite extra people over to a friend's party without asking permission. We only tell the hosts at the door, like, "Merry Christmas! Here's my brother's family, too—come in, Walter and Betty, boys . . . there are four daughters here, maybe you can meet them, go inside now, go . . ." It all went down with a super big smile while my parents stood there frozen. My mom actually looked extra-frozen because she was calculating whether there was enough ham for five more teenagers. And quietly seething with a gritted smile, where only her offspring could tell that the surprise of the moment might surely come out in some later meltdown. But looking back, who could blame her?

Christmas was usually fifty. Thanksgiving was the same deal: fifty. It was always our big house, large trays of dumplings, a Honey Baked Ham for $5,000 or whatever, and my ice bucket with the cool clear plastic tongs that I got to use to fill it up. My holiday hosting job? Punch management. Orange sherbet, 7-Up, and the frozen cylinder of Minute Maid. We should've basically rented a fire hose connected to a syrup vat and stood people in line with open mouths.

Growing up in an immigrant church community meant everything was a massive potluck, a reason for bigger, fuller, and more. A theology of *God helped us survive the war and even gave us leftovers*, if you will. We ate in folding chairs in a circle without a table, because who had time for formal table settings? You shoveled in noodles before happily scampering back to the counter for garlicky green beans and crunchy bits of ham. Punch cups at our feet, adults in some other room talking about their things, and all of us eventually dissipating to board games before the eventual call to the piano to sing.

My mom printed out the holiday song lyrics the week before on her own Xerox machine. She put them in folders sometimes, with "CHRISTMAS CAROLS" in her neat capital letters atop each first page. We were like our own kickass Staples store, in fact, complete with drawer units to hold the special paper plates, plastic cutlery, and lyrics folders. Every holiday, every year.

So when Easter 2018 rolled around, on April Fool's no less, I was struck with how differently I was preparing for it. Maybe one reason is that I'm getting married this year. So my fiancé, three sons, and I are all in the middle of that premarital soup of second marriages, complete with pre-parenting and pre-routining home life and pre-ritualizing holidays. There are different players in the room now, who are all in our little dance of getting to know you/them/us/him/her/ourselves. Even the kids are each ever in flux, one day as stable as argon gas, the next a fricking mess. We're all more or less religious, so we did some holiday exercises that we've done in some form together before; they were a definite highlight. But the bottom line is, things are uncharted. What makes for a good day, a "successful celebration," whatever that is, is developing.

Maybe a second reason this holiday felt different is that I'm no longer in a job where holidays are assumed to be busy. When I was an associate pastor, the lead-up to a holiday had to do more with the church calendar and much less about our family's calendar. My mind was on my notes for a sermon, or supply list for a kid activity, or laminating the 150 homemade Mother's Day magnets that still needed to have the magnet back glued on. My assumption was that communal celebrations and my family's observances were really one and the same. Joy was big, people were central, and love was better experienced in the diversity of many families, many individuals, many stories.

I still sometimes love all that big communal stuff, especially in a fractured world where peaceful, diverse crowds speak of something better and higher. But now, my daily work life is very contained. True, I'm still a school parent, a local business even, if you count neighborhood piano teachers as local business people. So there's at least a habit of awareness that our calendar and goodwill concerns ought to extend beyond our closest circle. But, as basic as it sounds, I never quite understood the phrase "my family and friends" in the sweet, intimate way some people use it. I sort of thought, *Of course*, but then immediately asked, *"And who else besides them?"*

I didn't ask about anyone else's needs and wants besides my own family's this year. This year, in the weeks leading up to the holiday, we decided to do activities like writing each other nice notes. Those nights we had time, we ripped up paper into slips and passed them around the table, writing in silence punctuated by occasional snickers. Then we'd read them aloud and laugh if everyone repeated the same thing to the same person like, "Good job washing the dishes." But during the forty days before Easter, we settled into this rhythm of really considering each other. What did we notice? What did we appreciate? What could we call out about each other, in this thing we were forming called family? Fights that inevitably erupted became slips of paper that expressed appreciation for fights resolved. Dreams that had mixed emotions for everyone came up. Deep observations about each other alternated with emerging inside jokes, both profound for their intimate "it stays here" nature. By Easter's eve, one boy remarked, "What I really liked was that we had conversations that would be totally different if someone else was in the room. It was just us." And in balance, we pondered how we could also relate well with wider circles of friends and those we don't yet know.

What about the endless potluck feast of all the holidays we'd celebrated before? The boys had begged for grilled lamb kebobs. The weather would be warm enough, they argued, with that charming denial of New Englanders forgetting April snow showers.

"Please don't make stewed lamb," Stephen said, making "stewed" sound like it'd be steamed on erasers.

They had a point, though. Grilled meat would be fun and tasty and wouldn't break the bank if I bought three pounds instead of thirteen. But I wasn't familiar with how to do it, and I already wanted to make something else that was new—a white cake with fancy layers. Also, grilling seemed to have a right way and a charred way. Cakes? They become cardboard if you just leave it in one minute too long or slide off the plate if you assemble one minute too early.

Anyway, the risk of saying yes to the meal request loomed symbolically larger than just figuring out whether the grill gas line was still in working order. It seemed to proclaim that my effort and time for my little nuclear family's desires was bigger than basically anything else I was doing that holiday. There was no hosting of others. No audience of many. No emails to coordinate arrivals and departures, potluck contributions or programmed moments of speaking. Just five people, an explicit preference for grilled meat, and my desire to bake a cake.

The day came, and we went to church in time to get coffee and sit in our dress-up clothes. I had even taken enough time to decide that the first outfit I'd put on wasn't quite right, so I changed to another. I walked, not sprinted, down the stairs, and simply followed my family out the door without yelling for help to carry five bags of supplies with us. We worshiped, then sent Sam to the car with a headache to wait for us without panicking that he'd have to sweat it out for three more hours while we hosted hundreds for a reception after the service. We chatted briefly with friends we like, then drove home. Sam took some ibuprofen and a nap. And then James made the potatoes and fired up the grill, and I assembled my layer cake and the kebobs. After we ate, we cleared the table, sat on our couches, and talked and prayed about Easter and Jesus-y stuff.

That night, James said to me that it was the best Easter he'd had in a very long time. And I couldn't help but think of another ancient proverb that says it's better to have a crumb in a house of peace than a house of feasting but with strife. Yes, I nodded to myself, the "crumbs" of those complimentary slips of paper and streamlined meal turned out amazingly fulfilling. And moreover, I saw the people sitting right in front of me, really saw them and then saw them again. And maybe for one of the first times ever on a holiday, the joy was biggest in the smallest circle.

A Note to Disneyland

November 2018

Dear Disneyland,

I'm writing to say goodbye. It's hard to do this because you've lived in my head for a long, long time now. I can still see the Matterhorn peak from my early consciousness as my sisters and I craned our necks to spot our favorite roller coaster mountain, approaching from Interstate 5's off-ramp. Behind Motel 6, some skinny palm trees, and several layers of restaurants ready to take advantage of tourists—there you were. A promise of imaginative lands and creative thrills for fifteen hours.

You were my first real boyfriend. I used to pause in the parking lot and say to you, if it all ends suddenly, I'm still glad I saw you that day. No joke: I trusted you that much to treat me well. I had great confidence in our ability to make a great day together and accepted the fact that, even if an emergency drove us out of the park early, I would still fare better that we'd come for a bit than if we'd missed our reunion altogether.

In terms of thrills, you definitely didn't disappoint. We of course followed the Chang sisters' best route, where anybody who was anyone started in Tomorrowland, skipping "old people" amusements such as elaborate window dressings on Main Street. We flew by those, snubbing the horse-drawn carriages, and landed in line for Adventures through Inner Space. Looking at the caravan of blue chairs on that ascending conveyor belt, I swear I resisted the urge to bid my mom goodbye forever, knowing that soon I'd get in a blue chair and be shrunk to molecular size and zoom billions of miles away.

The building of Space Mountain perfectly coincided with my growing up. In the late 70s, we got this indoor speed coaster, completely in the dark save for the glowing asteroid that looked like a giant chocolate chip cookie. By 1979, I believe this was the ride my entire visit hinged on, the one where at the end of our long day my compatriots and I would ask each other, "How many times?" One time, and you were issued a check of satisfaction. Twice, score. And three times, well, that means you'd managed the end-of-night sprint back to be careened at high speed once more. Totally rad.

The secrets of the "Happiest Place on Earth" were later revealed in books that shared cool details like the underground passageways, where un-costumed staff could quickly traverse the grounds without distracting from visitors' magic. Trash pick-up from tens of thousands of daily visitors? Invisible, carried down hatched stairways to those tunnels and emptied in dumpsters outside the park. Flower beds within the park were deadheaded every day at dawn so the rising sun greeted perfect blooms sporting no fade. Painters made the rounds in a continuous circuit round your buildings and rides, leaving no character or ceiling beam peeling. Those same books also exposed darker truths, like exclusive practices that barred those from employment who didn't fit the clean-cut stereotype. Earrings above the lobe. Men's hair, clear of the neck. Tattoos? Forget it. It was years before my awareness of those restrictions connected with knowledge of corporations' worship of some cultural norms and denigration of others. At the time, I was too enamored with cannons in pirates' caves and flying high atop Dumbo the Elephant.

Given all I've been through now, I'm humbled to acknowledge how deeply I attached to your theme park and each narrative you dished up for a happy ending. For my first honeymoon, it was not insignificant, for example, that Andrew and I spent a full day on your grounds in Anaheim, en route to California's northern coast. Though I didn't tell him in such words, the little girl in me felt delighted that my true love had hung out with me in my true hometown. Each ride had its three-minute cycle of crisis and resolution, far outpacing Hollywood's two hours. Snow White? The witch offered the poisoned apple, but round the corner and you were dancing with the maiden and her seven dwarves. The Matterhorn? The Abominable Snowman roared at our bobsled as we flew past, but a few turns up and down and we were splashing through water to a safe stop. Even Adventure through Inner Space held our fates in the balance for a spare few moments, wherein our descent to molecules bumped us on ice crystals but returned us to Earth human-sized again. We escaped pirates' fires, hippopotamuses, falling rocks, and haunted mansions. And the best part was, we ended our stay each time with fried chicken and dime candy sticks from the cart in New Orleans Square.

There was never fuss during the day for expensive ice cream, or complaints over long lines. I never needed gift store trinkets or more sugar on our way out. Indeed, the commercialism parents love to hate about you entirely failed to woo me. Instead, the fantasy of happiness itself was so ingrained in my soul that sugar cravings were an afterthought. I simply basked in a theology that God makes it all better, quickly, and with color and music. After all, weren't we in the Magic Kingdom? Every visit, I exited down Main Street to the parking lot tram, satisfied that justice had been served to every heroine and healing for every orphaned animal I'd seen. The notion that hope or faith required patience or that shit can hit the fan for years, as I now know it can, eluded me.

So now, as I bid you farewell, my dear childhood knight in shining armor, my eyes well up with sadness to let you go, with your freshly trimmed floral beds and dancing birds on a stage. I'm grateful for the innocent surrender you offered me. It was, as was my first taste of religious faith, infused with goodness, freedom, and creative fun. I don't regret any of my scampering happily through your lands, believing that all the good overcame all the evil. Something in me still holds on to the belief that bad things—death, betrayal, loss, and failure— will resolve in some kind of forever deal for the universe, complete with real smiles.

A consolation occurred to me upon one visit during my teen years, and I treasure this memory as truth. It took place in your Adventureland as I stood still. When my cousin Joanne and I waited one summery dusk in the Temple of Doom line, I glanced up to the ceiling and observed stars on the darkened canvas. "How impressive," I commented to my cousin. "The painters did an amazing job; it looks so much like the real night sky." And she answered that it was in fact the real night sky. Stunned to silence, I focused my gaze upward again and confirmed her claim. I could feel the evening breeze on my face, and I realized our line had wandered outside the building, with nothing barring us from the warm summer air. In that moment of revelation, I filed away this thought that reality was more impressive and captivating than artificial beauty and light.

I call to mind that consolation once again.

Acknowledgments

Thank You

This book is a product of many encouraging nudges from loved ones as well as thirty-seven years of journal keeping.

In 2013, my friends Will Crosby and Kathy Simmonds held a reading in their home so I could share my first chapters with a supportive audience. About twenty-five friends attended, and I was honored that they laughed, nodded, or cried as I read aloud my memories of first diagnoses and first dates. This gathering encouraged me to assemble the stories for publication.

My husband James, upon reading the draft manuscript, noticed the absence of several very important reflections, which are now included. Most notably, he urged me to put into writing the saddest piece of my story to date, that of Andrew's death day. I can't say I felt better afterward, but I am very thankful I faced the music to put that experience into words. Moreover, I deeply appreciate the space James has given me and our family to honor Andrew and continue to grieve our losses as we forge a life together.

My sons Sam, Stephen, and Mark have put up with curious questions and stares from our loving villages of friends and family for their entire lives. I gratefully acknowledge their tolerance and forgiveness in having their stories spilled in church sermons or writing. Of course, they have their own take on things, and my stories should not overshadow their version of how life has gone.

To my beloved Jamaica Plain peeps, the Curley K-8 School, the extended Chang and Snekvik families, and the Stanford Park Boulevard circle: they are the best communities in which to receive a diagnosis one day and have to do kindergarten drop-off the next morning. I'm thankful for folks listening to us, praying lots, driving Andrew to appointments, coming to the funeral, reaching out to love the boys, teaching and coaching them, taking me out to drink, cooking for us, filling out dating profiles, hiring the boys for jobs, and most recently, supporting our new adventures of all kinds.

The Children's Room in Arlington, Massachusetts was a unique offering for grieving families at the time. The boys and I spent two years driving across town through rush hour traffic twice a month, to sit in a room with our peers. Why? I think we craved the utter sanity to know we weren't alone, crazy, pathetic, or hopeless. Or maybe, it was so that when we felt those ways, it was also okay. Also, we laughed a lot.

The Reservoir Church in Cambridge, MA, and other faith communities past and present helped shape the essence of whatever is hopeful in this book. I still trust that there is a God who's alive and who loves and leads us when we ask, including in tragedy and all kinds of societal crazy times. So for that, I'm deeply affectionate towards sincere love of the religious kind. And many faith-filled friends embody that love in rare and inspiring form.

To Kerri Miller, my editor: her astute eyes and experience went to work, making sure my manuscript was polished. As a novice, I felt very comforted knowing she helped me follow standard writing practice wherever needed. And bits of her story, as revealed in her comments, underscored my hunch that many of us share common experience more than we all think.

To Susanna Chapman, my cover art designer: I am amazed I can say her artwork is the image people will see when they first encounter the book. After fawning over Susanna's exquisite, emotive drawings for years, I immediately thought of her when pondering who could capture complex experiences in one simple set of images. I'm grateful for her tender, thoughtful way of approaching my stories.

It is my sincere regret that I cannot list all those who have directly or indirectly contributed to this book. Several people used their professional and practical skills to buoy my family this last decade and deserve special mention: Karen Argetsinger, whose productive skills as a lawyer are matched by her warm hospitality; Maureen Conway, my tax accountant who filled significant gaps of knowledge around Social Security when I was newly widowed; my former colleague Joanne Turner, who spent hours on and beyond her job time organizing my personal files, passwords, and accounts so I wouldn't have to; and Mary Urban Keary, whose feedback as a therapist has reassured me that there is life after Disneyland.